'Charm and enthusiasm, ... chance, warmth and una... and humour cascade from between the lines . . . He drove as he lived, and it cheers you to read about it'   Alan Judd, *Sunday Telegraph*

'Anyone who enjoys the Clark prose style, indeed anyone who has ever had a zest for life . . . will find reading *Back Fire* a thrill from cover to cover. The breadth of vision that made his historical and political books best-selling insights into the undaunted spirit of man is present on every page . . . an essential read for the dedicated motor-maniac, but also a joy for the ambling boulevardier whose reflection, be assured, speedily receded into an insignificant dot in the great man's wing mirror'   Graham Stewart, *Spectator*

'A book . . . to pick up and savour like a fine wine from Clark's cellar, or a large glass of malt in the library of Eriboll on a winter's afternoon'   Stuart Somerville, *Scotsman*

'A collection of writings inspired by the serial adulterer's most passionate affair . . . There is a wide enough variety of subject matter here to delight the connoisseur and appal the easily offended . . . a rich concoction, charting the extravagant views and flamboyant style of a great diarist and irrepressible human being'
Stephen Picton, *Driving Magazine*

'A brilliant book for the real motoring enthusiast. Leave prejudices at home and you will be seduced as Clark always intended'
Campbell Spray, *Independent on Sunday*

'In this fascinating and thought-provoking book he comes across as a man in love with the past, personified by cars where inspiration, craftsmanship and dedication combined in a trinity of hand, mind and eye. They don't make them like that any more'
James Leasor, *The Oldie*

'*Back Fire* is an entertaining read that enthusiasts will enjoy dipping into . . . some great anecdotes . . . Good fun'   *Classic & Sports Car*

'A fascinating read for all motoring enthusiasts'   *Vintage Roadscene*

'If you have read Alan Clark's inimitable *Diaries*, this book will prove to be irresistible – it reads as though it were a long Cars in the Life of— article ... a fascinating story, too; it even includes Clark's instructions for disposal of his collection after his death'

The Automobile

Alan Clark, MP for Plymouth (Sutton) 1974–92 and Kensington and Chelsea 1997–9, was Minister of Trade, 1986–9, and Minister of State, Ministry of Defence, 1989–92. He was married with two sons and lived at Saltwood Castle, Kent. Following his death in 1999, a second volume of his journals – *Diaries: Into Politics* – was published in 2002, with a third and final volume, *The Last Diaries*, following in October 2003.

Robert Coucher, the editor, commissioned Alan Clark's 'Back Fire' column for *Classic Cars* magazine, which he edited between 1994 and 1998. Coucher contributes a monthly column to the magazine, as well as occasional features. He writes on classic cars for the *Daily Telegraph*. Like Alan Clark, he is a firm believer in keeping classic cars well exercised, not just well polished.

BY ALAN CLARK

FICTION

Bargains at Special Prices

Summer Season

The Lion Heart: a tale of the war in Vietnam

NON-FICTION

The Donkeys: a History of the BEF in 1915

The Fall of Crete

Barbarossa: The Russian–German Conflict, 1941–45

Aces High: the War in the Air over the Western Front, 1914–1918

A Good Innings: the private papers of Viscount Lee of Fareham (*edited*)

Suicide of the Empires: The Eastern Front, 1914–1918

Diaries: In Power 1983–1992

The Tories: Conservatives and the Nation State, 1922–1997

Diaries: Into Politics 1972–1982 (*edited by Ion Trewin*)

Back Fire: A passion for cars and motoring

The Last Diaries: In and Out of the Wilderness
(*edited by Ion Trewin*)

Back Fire

A passion for cars and motoring

ALAN CLARK

Edited and with an Introduction
by Robert Coucher

PHOENIX

A PHOENIX PAPERBACK

First published in Great Britain in 2001
by Weidenfeld & Nicolson
This paperback edition published in 2002
by Phoenix,
an imprint of Orion Books Ltd,
Orion House, 5 Upper St Martin's Lane,
London WC2H 9EA

A CIP catalogue record for this book
is available from the British Library.

ISBN 0 75381 373 4

Typeset by Selwood Systems, Midsomer Norton

Printed and bound in Great Britain by
Clays Ltd, St Ives plc

'Ever tried driving the whole way to Gleneagles at 100 mph in an open car? On arrival the tip of your nose will be bright red, the passenger will want to wash her hair at once, and there will be a strange ringing sound in your skull that will persist all through dinner.'

Alan Clark, August 1996

Contents

Illustrations

The photographs included are from the Clark family albums

The first motoring photograph to capture an image of Alan Clark behind the wheel – in his 2½ litre Jaguar SS100.

His beloved Jaguar XK120 which was bought new in November 1950 from City Motors in Oxford.

The Volkswagen Beetle pictured with Jane in 1958, the year they married.

Enjoying a Ferrari 750 Monza on the Abetone pass.

An early snap of Jane and son James with the Ford coupé.

Alan's pale blue Fifties Oldsmobile which appears to have a British Automobile Racing Club badge mounted on the front bumper.

The Mercedes 600 on one of the many trips to the chalet in Zermatt, Switzerland.

Alan competing in the Jaguar XK120. The car has its full-width windscreen fitted.

The Citroën 2CV, or 'the Mickey' as it was affectionately known.

A Willys Jeep bought when the Clarks lived in Devon.

The Austin Seven saloon known as 'Ruby'.

'Until you have driven a Talbot Lago your motoring experience is incomplete,' noted Alan of this fearsome 1947 Talbot Lago single-seater racing car.

The 'winter car', one of the Clarks' two 1967 Chevrolet Impalas.

Victory day at Silverstone Circuit, April 1969. The big black Mercedes 600 is parked next to the 'Bira' Bentley.

Alan Clark in action driving his first 1923 Rolls-Royce Silver Ghost in the 1973 Great Alpine Rally; and at rest in a car park.

Two Derby Bentleys.

A line-up of Bentley Continentals at Saltwood.

This 1937 Rolls-Royce Phantom III was once the property of the Maharajah of Jaipur.

The original 'John Player Special', a 1937 Rolls-Royce 25/30.

Alan bought his Rolls-Royce Silver Shadow solely for the number plate – AC 1800.

Alan's 1910 chain-driven Locomobile.

'Little Silver', the Porsche 911 Carrera Cabriolet which he collected new from the factory in Stuttgart in 1985.

This 1957 Porsche 550A Spyder was Porsche-works driver von Frankenburg's own car.

The 1936 Buick Phaeton straight eight is kept on the Eriboll estate.

The fully-loaded Discovery going off piste somewhere in Scotland.

Trying to squeeze the Citroën 2CV into his father's Saltwood garden house.

Grandson Albert behind the wheel of the little Citroën Mehari.

Jane's lovely Citroën DS Decapotable, one of only 1,365 ever built by specialist Henri Chapron; and on one of the Hamilton Rallies.

The 8-litre Bentley with Vanden Plas bodywork.

James Clark at the wheel of a Bentley 4½.

Charles Howard's AMG rally in July 1989. Alan's Jaguar SS100 is second from left.

Seen here in white livery, this 1955 D-type Jaguar was later repainted black.

Three Jaguars outside Saltwood: SS100, SS100 and XK120.

The Ferrari 340MM coupé which he bitterly regretted not buying.

Alan driving one of his favourite cars – his 1920 Rolls-Royce Silver Ghost – on the 1993 Rolls-Royce Enthusiasts' Club Alpine commemorative run.

Returning from the Alpine, Alan awaits the Hovercraft back to Saltwood.

A favourite photograph of Jane's: Alan sitting in the Ghost, during the Alpine rally, in thoughtful mood.

The Silver Ghost in 'barn find' storage, providing a good perch for the Saltwood peacocks before being rebuilt.

The Rolls-Royce Silver Ghost's Bat mascot.

Another firm favourite, a 1953 Bentley R-type Continental.

This was the first of Alan's new Bentley Continentals, a Continental R finished in a subtle shade of Queen Mother claret.

A very rare 1958 Bentley Continental S1, this was the last car to leave Crewe with a manual gearbox.

As patron of the XK Club Alan hosted a Jaguar meeting at Saltwood in July 1999.

A photograph taken just to annoy the purists! A combined weight of over 200lbs of prime Rottweiler on top of the thin aluminium bodywork of the C-type Jaguar.

The C-type being comprehensively climbed upon by much of the Clark family.

The Rottweilers in the rear of the Bentley 4½ with Jane.

Another favourite, the now rather bedraggled looking 1956 Volkswagen.

Spring 1999, Alan and 'the girls' in Big Red.

Acknowledgements

The Editor wishes to thank the following for their assistance in preparing this volume: Jane Clark, James Clark, Dr Michael Coucher, Ivor Gordon, John Fasal, Charles Howard, Christian Hueber, Peter Tomalin, Ion Trewin, Jack Barclay Ltd., the Rolls-Royce Enthusiasts' Club, *CAR Magazine*, *Classic Cars*, *Daily Telegraph*, *Financial Times*, *Private Motor Car Collections of Great Britain* by Peter Hugo, *Road & Track*, *Jaguar World*, *Superclassics*.

Alan Clark's diary entries are taken from the two published volumes, *Diaries: in Power* and *Diaries: into Politics* as well as his unpublished motoring journals.

Introduction Robert Coucher

Strong views and detailed knowledge

One of the best things I did as the editor of *Classic Cars* magazine was to persuade Alan Clark to contribute a monthly column. 'Back Fire', as his piece was called, was initially on the last page of the magazine, hence its title. Alan particularly liked its location opposite a colour advertisement that was usually for an upmarket Bentley and Rolls-Royce dealer.

Because of its position, his column was easily found in the magazine and was invariably what most of our readers turned to first. His brief was to be controversial and he certainly was. Alan elicited more correspondence than all the other contributors put together. But more often than not, readers would respond positively to what he wrote about, because he would stir their memories of the great motor cars and epic drives that they had experienced in the past.

Certainly, there were those who thought he was an opinionated, spoilt, right-wing snob and, when he felt like it, he would willingly foist that perception upon the reader. But most classic car enthusiasts reading the magazine thought he was great because he actually did the sort of things with exciting cars that most of us can only dream about. He was a dashing young blade, flouting the rules of convention and getting away with it. He bought his first car while still at Eton in 1946, a 6½ litre Vintage Bentley, an outrageous machine for such a young learner driver. This was followed by a Jaguar SS100 and then his first new car, a Jaguar XK120, bought in November 1950 from the showrooms of City Motors in Oxford where he was an undergraduate.

This conjures up an image of a time when it was a genuine pleasure to drive classic sports cars. It was romantic, exciting and a little dangerous, but those were the days when sports cars were used for real motoring. And motoring is what Alan always enjoyed immensely. In 1948 he drove his SS100 from London to the Isle of Skye in Scotland and these were the days prior to motorways. He then chased the sun in Europe, driving his XK120 around France and Italy, up various challenging mountain passes through the Alps. Borrowing Ferraris for test drives and attaching himself to a ballet company – a great way to meet athletic young women – he was free and leading what must have been a charmed existence. The Jaguar was being enjoyed to the full when he started courting Jane, soon to be his wife. She remembers the wonderful sound of the six-cylinder engine preceding Alan's arrival when he came to visit. Later he drove his little Citroën 2CV all the way to the house in Zermatt; journeys to the Continent and Scotland became a regular event in the Clark household, and were embarked upon in a range of machines as diverse as a gargantuan Mercedes 600 and a thrifty diesel Land-Rover Discovery.

Alan's tales were always backed up by detailed mechanical knowledge. He knew a good car when he saw one and was not a car snob; he would get just as enthusiastic about his battered old Volkswagen Beetle as he would about his magnificent Rolls-Royce Silver Ghost. Try as he might, he could not help himself; he vociferously extolled the very best of British traits – always championing the underdog. As is apparent in his *Diaries*, in the early days he had experienced being hard up and he resorted to buying and selling cars, even spending time at London's notorious secondhand car centre of the period in Warren Street, off the Tottenham Court Road. Before he became an MP in 1975, there was so much trading going on at Saltwood Castle that it was soon dubbed Saltwood Cars Sales. And that's what the readers loved: expansive motoring experiences, an enviable understanding of engineering, an educated grasp of history, a wide interest in all sorts of machines as well as enough outrageous anecdotes to make even the most crusty cynic roar with laughter. Here was Mr Toad personified.

It is apparent to anyone reading him that Alan loved driving original cars. He could not abide machines that had been stripped and rebuilt thus losing their essential and irreplaceable originality and patina. Growing up at Saltwood Castle and being surrounded by his father's collection of art and antiquities made a lasting impression. Throughout this book you will find him banging on about how cars are destroyed by restoration, and I think he is right. His good friend Charles Howard, the Rolls-Royce and Bentley specialist and excellent backgammon player, says, only half jokingly, that Alan was just plain mean and couldn't bring himself to spend hard cash on a car's bodywork. In Alan's defence, he always tried to ensure his cars were mechanically on the button, even going so far as to persuade the Jaguar factory to rebuild completely his XK for the tough Carrera Panamericana road-race through Mexico.

In the very first 'Back Fire' column Alan lambastes the American restorers who hold a very grand Concours d'Elégance every year at Pebble Beach golf club in Monterey, California. Here the cars are trophies, they are rarely driven and hundreds of thousands of dollars are spent on them as part of a ritualistic ego match. This sort of excess annoyed Alan and he said so. From day one the letters flowed which from my point of view was a good thing. One American reader posted an enema pack to the magazine to be forwarded on to him. Alan thought this was terrifically funny and said it proved that our cousins across the Atlantic do have a sense of humour.

Occasionally, Alan would overdo it and write something insensitive. When he suggested that the electrical systems of Italian cars 'appear to have been assembled by handicapped children in a Unicef hostel', a number of readers were upset. Afterwards he was sorry he had caused offence and this was characteristic of his enigmatic nature. He could be cruel, yet he was anti-hunting and would only eat meat that had not been through an abattoir. On one occasion, when a car he was selling was delivered from Saltwood to a London dealer, a small field mouse jumped out and scuttled down the mews. When told, Alan was anguished at the thought of the poor mouse being doomed to city life in central London.

Alan was well known by the London dealers in the various mews around Queen's Gate in Kensington. He was notorious for striking a hard bargain and on more than one occasion he would play backgammon for the couple of thousand pounds' price differential in a deal, losing more often than not. He was also known to take the batteries out of cars before selling them. For a time, or while he could get away with it, he kept a couple of old smokers that he was trading, usually Bentleys or Rolls-Royces, in the parking lot under the Houses of Parliament. 'Cheapest parking in central London,' he remembered in all seriousness. Commons officials were not amused.

Initially it took some persuasion to get Alan to write the 'Back Fire' column and I felt certain he would soon tire of it. I would call him every month to chat about what was being featured in the magazine. At first he would be short and impatient so I learnt to call his secretary to find out when would be the best time to talk to him. After a while, when the column was obviously being well received, Alan relaxed and became more enthusiastic. If I got him after a good lunch he'd be positively ebullient, and talkative, almost writing the column on the phone. I'm sure his detailed knowledge of Vintage cars, racing in the 1950s and the names of obscure villages in the Alps was lodged in his brain – he seldom needed, or could be bothered, to look things up. When he made mistakes he would own up in print, but that only happened twice.

At one point things went sour because the magazine's accounts department would not pay Alan in the way he wanted, as our system was not to his liking. There was a spat so I sent him a placatory case of wine. The bill gave my publisher apoplexy, but the ploy worked and Alan was appreciative. Recently, doing some research at Saltwood, I came across the letter I enclosed with the wine. In the margin he had scribbled down the price, obviously having called the merchant to find out exactly how much we spent on him!

He was further encouraged to continue contributing 'Back Fire' when, as he later told me, he was approached when walking through the Palace of Westminster, by a senior foreign diplomat who offered his congratulations. Alan was amazed that the magazine was read by dignitaries of such stature.

In June 1998 *Classic Cars* were hosting an awards evening at

Goodwood House near Chichester with Alan as the guest of honour. He arrived late and eschewed the dress rehearsal, preferring to have a look around the classic cars auction being set up for the next day. So he, Jane and I climbed into his Bentley Continental S, a special order car which he had had built to his requirements. Arriving at the entrance to the grounds, we found ourselves on the start of the Goodwood Festival of Speed hillclimb. Alan's eyes lit up. He stopped on the line, selected first gear and floored the throttle. As this was the set-up day before the event there were people milling about all over the place, climbing ladders to fit bunting and lugging straw bales. The roaring leviathan of a Bentley, going flat out up the driveway, scattered the startled workers with Alan chuckling all the way.

Later that evening when Sir Stirling Moss was presented with an award, he was impressed with Alan's encyclopaedic knowledge of his many race victories. Alan recounted the story when, as a young man behind the wheel of his SS100 Jaguar, he came across a fast-driven BMW 328. He did his best to stay level with the BMW but, much to his annoyance, he couldn't get anywhere near. He later discovered that the driver was none other than Stirling Moss, so he regarded that as perfectly acceptable. Jane appeared to be totally relaxed about Alan's colourful and exuberant past, and she laughed about a time when driving out of Saltwood Castle she found the press encamped by the gates. She was off to collect Alan from Sandling station after he had been in the papers once again, and, to avoid the cameras, he hid in the boot. Arriving home, she said she was almost tempted to leave him in there.

Alan really loved his diverse collection of cars, and his moss-green 1953 Bentley R-type Continental was a firm favourite. He was an original, in that his Continental was magnificently scruffy, even dirty, clearly not having been washed for decades. But that's how he liked his cars; it was inverted snobbery, really, as clean cars imply you care too much. When we had the chance to look at his Jaguars, Rolls-Royce and other Bentleys, I noticed his Porsche 911 had a dent on the front wing. I ran my hand along the bruised flank and Alan responded by saying he had no intention of repairing it. Genteel decrepitude was his thing. Of course this is a lot cheaper than keeping a collection of cars in pristine condition. Even the Silver Ghost is shabby with virtually no bodywork fitted at all.

Back Fire is a collection of Alan Clark's thoughts and writings on cars and motoring over nearly half a century. Although the book draws extensively on the monthly 'Back Fire' columns that he wrote for *Classic Cars* magazine from July 1996 until just before his death on 5 September 1999, some pieces were written as long ago as 1951. A few have survived incomplete, but nothing has been intentionally altered. Sometimes, when his writing has proved illegible some editing has been necessary.

Other motoring excerpts from his diaries – some not previously transcribed – are also included. Because Alan wrote mainly about his personal experiences with cars, there is understandably a degree of repetition. Bentleys, Rolls-Royces, Porsches and women feature strongly, but he also exhibits a wider knowledge of some really obscure machines. Jaguar remains his favourite: 'fast and glamorous . . . open sesame with the girls'.

April 2001

Foreword James Clark

Always buying what he liked

Outside the family, I truly believe, cars were my father's greatest love.

He always told me that he followed his father's advice, probably for the only time: when collecting art, 'always buy what you like, not what you think you should have'.

He loved his cars to be original, preferably low mileage, but always with the patina of wear that conveyed to him the car's history. He abhorred 'Connollising', as he referred to it – the restoration of a car and in particular the reupholstering of seats in coloured leather to such stiffness and shine as to be indistinguishable from some ghastly 1960s Hong Kong vinyl, so beloved these days by 'celebs' and 'nouves'. Many times on rallies, notably Kensington Gardens or even the Alpine, where 'rivet counters', sundry 'anoraks' and sour-faced old buffers would 'tut-tut' amongst themselves about his total disregard of the paint it, chrome it brigade.

That his cars always had names made them more personal and, I suppose, subconsciously therefore, harder to part with. A car that one knew of just as an open Derby Bentley was clearly trading stock and its days were numbered, on the other hand the 'Barnato' and the 'hen' were going to remain as part of the family.

The first car I remember was his Jaguar XK120, painted in Old English White. This was and still is known as 'the noisy car' on account of its modified engine (to C-type spec) and straight-through exhaust. My father had this car totally reworked before I was born to compete in the Carrera Panamericana, adding the racing engine, disc brakes and Koni shock absorbers all round and having the boot replaced by a Le Mans fuel tank. Fortunately he never entered. It would be an even bet that the car, which is now probably the only XK120 owned from new in the same hands, would be a twisted wreck slowly decaying in some Mexican backwoods with the possibility, more disturbingly, that I would not be writing this.

We moved from Bratton in Devon to Seend in Wiltshire in the 1960s and with it space became available. Although the old favourites came with us, more and more cars would arrive, and new buildings were built to house them.

The problem with 'covered space' never goes away, it is something you can never have enough of wherever you are in a country with a climate like ours. When we arrived at Saltwood in 1972, the first thing my father did was erect a ten-car garage. Later he bought a shop in the village for the sole reason that it has an eight-car garage at the back, and the building of covered space has gone on ever since. I clearly remember a fairly recent mournful discussion on the matter, during a walk, when we decided that even if we had a building the size of Boeing's Jumbo assembly plant in Washington it would sooner or later be filled.

More than thirty years later the wonderful smell of Castrol R takes me back to the long summer evenings in the Great Stable Yard at Seend. After endless crashing of gears, broken tow-ropes and general cursing, some wonderful racing engine would belch into life, emitting clouds of blue smoke with the aroma of motoring's most addictive and enduring oil.

It was at Seend too where I was taught to drive in the little Mickey, our Citroen 2CV, on the vast expanse of Keevil aerodrome. Aficionados of the type will remember it had a centrifugal clutch, so it was possible to drive away in gear with the clutch out, thereby learning clutch control only changing up and down, making the whole process far less daunting than many learners find.

Having mastered the 2CV I graduated to the blue Jeep, my father's M.38 which had come from Bratton with us. This Jeep had arrived from Iceland brand new in a box and was a rare model, technically a V35/U 'Jeep for Underwater Use', as the U.S. Department of Navy manual states. I have the original here (as I do the Jeep which is still doing duties over forty years later). Nowhere in its 135 pages, which describe all aspects of its complicated re-breather engine controls etc., is there one mention of how the driver is supposed to either stay in his seat or survive seven feet under water.

I was taught to drive the Jeep with meticulous precision, reversing, positioning etc., only later to find this was nothing to do with a doting father, rather the fact that I was always around. This saved him bellowing for my mother to come out and tow yet another dead vehicle around.

This period also saw the arrival of many wonderful cars from India, sometimes on car transporters, but I particularly remember the Maharajah of Jaipur's Phantom III that arrived in a huge packing case literally, well, the size of a Phantom III plus a bit. We opened it with hammers and axes and the smells of India (not to mention bugs and creepy crawlies) and of course the all-pervading odour of stale petrol promising so much to come, have lasted for ever. Also the memory of my younger brother who managed to get a six-inch nail clean through his gumboot and foot and, with the wood attached, was carted off to A&E when the horrors of what infection this case might contain were realised.

Another car that arrived at this time was the wreck of a Bentley Continental R-type. It had been stolen by joyriders who, having picked up some hitch hikers – presumably to help them read the signposts on their way home – then rolled the car at over 100 mph in the New Forest and the car was practically FUBAR. No-one lived.

My father had this modified some time later into the 'Bang Bang', as it was known. This was truly the most evil-handling car I have ever driven, with a propensity to break traction in any gear followed by an instantaneous spin. It made a 911 Turbo in the wet seem like a battery-operated invalid cart. I am sure this was down to the fact that the unmodified rear suspension, as it seemed, should have been carrying its share of a ton and a half of bodywork rather than the 200 lbs that was now there. I cannot honestly say I am sad that it is now languishing in one of the Saltwood garages without an engine. While the car has tried to kill me and others on numerous occasions since, as a wreck, I am sure it saved my brother and I from serious assault. We were, as small children are wont to do when their parents are away, throwing handfuls of gravel from the shelter of the drive gates into the main road, when an irate tourist who had had his windscreen broken came to remonstrate with us. He took one look at the ghastly wreck not thirty feet away and while deciding whether these grubby bairns had been recently bereaved gave us a chance to run to the great cedar and hide.

Our next and final move was to Saltwood. As always, covered space was a priority as the collection continued to grow. I was becoming more and more involved with the mechanical side of the machines, and reached the stage that I could strip and rebuild an SU carburettor in my sleep. My father always made me drive every car in order to understand each of their various intricacies and foibles. I well remember Von Frankenburg's Mille Miglia Porsche, the first 'little silver'. A truly go-kart-like car that had a special taxiing gear offset from the normal pattern. When questioning my father about this anachronism he explained the car was designed to race, not drive slowly and you only used the gear to leave the pit area.

One stable-mate of the Porsche was a Jaguar D-type. On still summer evenings my father used to take it out for a blast on his 'circuit'. I can still hear it now, burbling up the lanes, followed by the howl as it turned out onto the A20 and accelerated crazily up through the gears. One did not need to be an anorak to know the car was doing well into three figures through the kink on the flats above Kick Hill and one waited with bated breath for the screech of tyres and unmistakable crump of collapsing metal. He did manage to spin the Mercedes 230SL on that stretch for over 300 yards without doing any damage, except for his nerves, something of a record. So it was always a great relief going down to open the gates on his return. In 1993, I took the XKC 013 down to Le Mans for the anniversary of Jaguar's historic win. It was fabulous to tear round that great circuit just before the main race but a total nightmare to try and get out of the place later in the day.

On the way back to Calais an Aston DB3S came up behind

us, and as taught by my father, he was not going to overtake and we passed through many miles of northern France at highly illegal speeds to the jolly waves of people outside the restaurants and gendarmes alike. Only a fast-bottoming fuel gauge, as well as the fact that Julie, my wife to be, was almost winning the decibel count with the engine at high revs, forced me to stop at a garage. I was really struck, as I filled that enormous tank with fairly shaky hands, by how incredibly brave the racing drivers of that period were, no seat-belts and only wafer-thin aluminium round their lower half. So different from the pampered prima donnas in their carbon-fibre monocoques that abound today.

My father's collection, being so diverse, gave one a far better perception of automotive history than many other less varied ones and this often led to some surprises, notably, the perception that the Derby Bentley represented the pinnacle of 1930s motoring.

Here at Eriboll we have a beautiful 1937 Buick Convertible, which my father bought from Canada. It is totally original and very low mileage. The spare has never been fitted, and we both suspected the hood had never been down. The hood tonneau cover was unopened in its original wrapping in the boot. She is almost exactly the same size as the equivalent Derby but that is where the similarity ends. Her controls are beautifully harmonised, the car feels so much lighter, her handling and suspension are without fault. The great straight-eight engine is almost silent and turbine-like in its smoothness, she is truly a wonderful open tourer. The Derby on the other hand – and I have driven many – feels agricultural by comparison, with heavy controls, a jiggly ride and dodgy brakes, also, in almost every case, idiotically under-geared.

Now to the future and yet again the talk is of a car cull, to bring the collection down to a more manageable, and garageable size; in recent years these culls have been about as meaningful as a local council meeting. On one occasion after an endless discussion on whether the list should start with the six 'must keeps' or the six 'could goes' the telephone rang and my father returned a while later to announce he had bought another Derby, so meeting over.

Some, well, one or two, may go. I am not holding my breath. I love the cars, and to me, they will always be a mechanical memorial to my father and his astuteness in his choice.

Eriboll
April 2001

Some cars and related matters

Alan Clark often made lists, which he delighted in annotating. Here are two relating to cars and motoring (the location is Salt-wood except where stated, Eriboll being his estate in Scotland):

From *Diaries: into Politics* (1972–1982)

Wee Bob – mechanic to Christopher Selmes, a friend of many years' standing who had made a fortune in the City
The Mews – composite name for various vintage car dealers' establishments in Queen's Gate, London
Coys of Kensington – dealers in classic cars

600 – Mercedes
550A Spyder – Porsche ex von Frankenberg Mille Miglia
The black SS100 – Jaguar owned by AC since his undergraduate days
The 'little white' – Mercedes 230SL
K10 – 1979 Chevrolet
OLA – Datsun 240Z, belonging to James (elder son)
THEBUS – 'the bus' – Transit van
The Winter Car – 1967 Chevrolet Impala
Summer Car – 1967 Chevrolet Impala convertible
The Mickey – 2CV
Winifred – a little Morris 8 two-seater which, due to its extremely short wheelbase, fitted snugly into a far corner of the long garage.
Bang-Bang – R-type Bentley Continental, the only Continental to be recorded stolen in the 1950s. Written off, it was rebodied by Bradley Brothers into a cut-down two-seater.

Cherrybum – Vintage 3 litre Bentley

Osprey and Atco – lawn mowers at Saltwood

From *Diaries: in Power* (1983–1992)

SS100 – Jaguar owned by AC since his undergraduate days

Rolls-Royce Silver Ghost – the nicest of all to drive on a fine day if you are not in a hurry

The Porsche (aka the Little Silver) – used most often by AC when alone

The Citroën (aka the Chapron) – the Decapotable belonging to Jane and used only for holidays

The 2CV – another Citroën, used when in de-escalation mode

The 'Bustard' – a very old 4½ litre Bentley

The Loco – a chain-driven racing car of 1910

The 'Wee One' – an old Land-Rover, MoT failure, used at Eriboll

The Mehari – a little plastic truck with an air-cooled engine and a very light footprint used for clearing grass clippings and prunings from the gardens because it does not mark the lawn. A kind of mobile wheelbarrow

The Argocat – performs the same function at Eriboll, but will also go through peat bogs, and swim

BACK FIRE

First memories of motoring

This appears to be a piece Alan wrote for the Rolls-Royce Enthusiasts' Club in 1977, three years after he first became a Member of Parliament. It was certainly typed on House of Commons writing paper. It leads in with his first motoring memories and quickly moves on to his favourite hobbyhorse, saving Vintage or classic cars from being vandalized by restoration. Alan was, in fact, ahead of his time in his preference for unrestored cars no matter how shabby they were.

Practically my earliest memory of childhood is standing anxiously (I would have been about five or six years old) on the quayside at Inverewe, having disembarked from one of the MacBrayne steamers, and seeing the two Rolls-Royces that my grandfather had sent to meet us – one for the passengers and one for the luggage – coming along on the far side of the loch, raising dust clouds on the unmade highland roads. It must have been August because we never went there before the twelfth but, unlike my recollections in later life, it never seemed to rain in that month. The car that was used for luggage was, in fact, an early thirty horse power (30 hp) which had been converted into a barrel-sided shooting brake by Croall and, as far as I can recall, was somewhat abused by the staff. But the Hooper landaulette was a glorious car (I now realize it was one of the very earliest with the short-stroke engine and 'springing gear') and it gave devoted service for over a quarter of a century. There was also a Hooper Tourer that was sometimes driven in races round the park on my grandfather's estate in Suffolk. Alas, it went to Palestine in the war and was never seen again. My first experience of actually *driving* a Silver Ghost was a 1911 Ferguson-bodied Tourer with a three-speed gearbox, not owned by me but bought by a friend quite cheaply – although at the time it seemed monstrously expensive – and in very unrestored condition. As anyone who has any feeling for motor cars will confirm, there is no sensation comparable to that special wafting progression that a good Silver Ghost with a light body provides when the governor is being used intelligently. Even when the cars are worn down to the bone, as this one was, they still convey a special quality of durable obedience.

I begged him not to 'restore' it, but he did, provoked possibly by the criticisms of some of those taking part in the rallies to which he took the car. It is perfectly incredible to me that cars should be criticized for showing signs of the long and devoted service that they have provided, or even for the abuse to which ignorant owners have in the past subjected them. Still less that one club which prides itself on being more 'exclusive' than the RREC should actually refuse to accept venerable machinery as being 'not up to standard'. Far be it from me to suggest that if such 'standards' were applied to the *owners* there might be a substantial fall in the subscription income.

Anyway, in it went and all the lovely Ferguson leather was stripped out; and the enamel was rubbed away; and the nickel was replated. And the faithful engine which, although no longer silent, still retained all the factory clearances, affected only by time and friction and beautifully loose and fine like a Purdey twelve-bore that has been to the butts a thousand times, was stripped down. And after everything had been metalled and brushed and ground and reamed and so on, it was carefully reassembled and put back into the chassis (which had had the same treatment) and reclad with the body (which was now bright and shiny), and I drove it again. It was transformed, unrecognizable – and ghastly. The steering was stiff, the accelerator linkage erratic, the brakes out of balance, the water temperature too high. The leather was stiff and hard, the doors difficult to open or close, the surface of the nickel plating instead of being smooth and dull was shiny and pitted. I don't doubt that the car was very much more valuable but as a beautiful object, a noble artefact, it had suffered a serious setback. It had, in fact, undergone a complete character change, becoming a kind of status symbol whose main owner-satisfaction had to derive from the fact that it represented a £20,000 banker's draft – Charles won't like this bit – (now presumably more) on four wheels.

I know that comments on market trends have to be expressed with considerable diffidence, particularly as there are now several professionals active in this field who analyse all the auction results and so forth. But the editor has twice allowed me to express my opinion on this subject in the past (on the Phantom III in 1959 and the Derby Bentley in 1968), and reading through those articles after a gap of many years, I can find nothing to retract or that has not been justified by the passage of time. And so if the reader will allow me I shall feel free to intersperse my own views on the market with these highly personal reflections on the *best* Car In The World.

My first car, a Vintage Bentley, will be just the job

A Bentley 6½ litre – not a bad way to start a long and exciting motoring life! This is an amusing memoir of how Alan learnt to drive this huge and heavy machine, although it does not appear to be entirely complete because it suddenly jumps to his experiences with his Buick. What he fails to mention here is that he lost his licence driving the Buick, for the 'relatively trivial offence' of allowing a young woman to drive the car while sitting on his lap, leaving him free to operate the pedals.

The first car that I owned was a 6½ litre Bentley – not a 'speed six', I am afraid, but a model with a single updraught Smith carburettor, that sucked the petrol in all right but did not seem to use it very efficiently once the mixture was in the combustion chamber, giving rise to a consumption of 8 mpg – hardly balanced by a maximum speed of 73 mph. It was a fine-looking car, though, with a Mulliner two-seater body with dicky; very well built with surprisingly good brakes, a flexible top-gear performance and, of course, the eternal delight of that long, pointed bonnet and burbling resonant exhaust note.

I bought this car while on 'long leave' in the middle of my last term at Eton. That was in the summer of 1946 when prices were really spiralling. I was young, and pretty idiotic, I suppose, and showed it. At any rate the dealer sank his teeth in and gave me the full treatment, even down to telling me the mileage was 33,000 – 'It's not run *in* yet, old chap,' – when in fact the odometer read 83,000 but the car was right at the back of a dark garage and the light was such that shadow obscured the first and last digits. Of course he refused to allow the car on the road for a trial, feigning monstrous indignation at the thought: 'My dear good fellow, the man who is going to buy that car has only got to set eyes on it. He'll hand me the money in pound notes right here at this office before he even walks across the garage floor to start her up.' My own position was the weaker for not yet possessing a driving licence.

However, once some minor adjustments had been made, the car proved to be not so bad. It stood up to my driving for several weeks. This, I should say, was entirely self-taught, from *watching* other people. Watching them fiddling about with the pedals and gear lever, that is, because as far as roadcraft went I knew all the answers. The whole thing was to accelerate, wasn't it? Particularly round corners? At low-speed manoeuvrability, however, I wasn't so hot, never having mastered the principle of slipping the clutch. When the pedal was pressed down nothing happened. OK, but when I took my foot off, the engine often stalled. Very humiliating. So the answer, it seemed, was to give the engine lots of gas just before letting go. This meant that the old car, weight nearly three tons, fairly heaved about in traffic, and with the infinitesimal delay imposed by the servo braking system – well!

That Buick was really a superlative machine, beautifully made, very strong, and with an extraordinary top-gear performance that would take the car from a standstill to just about a hundred. I bought it from an American undergraduate; nobody had paid any duty on the car so it had only had a short life in this country – although the very mild result of such a flagrant breach of the Customs regulations fostered an illusory sense of confidence over such matters that was to get me into serious trouble later.

I have many happy, and some mixed, recollections of this car. The first day that I had it, I got involved in a nasty dice with a Triumph Tiger 100 in Windsor Great Park of all places. He won but was, I like to think, as frightened as me and all my six passengers. Later that day there was a slight accident with a lorry in Eton High Street.

The car also played a part in the famous 'Napoleonic dinner' at the Roebuck in Oxford. Somebody else drove it in the parade that preceded this disastrous orgy, held on 11 June 1948, in the midst of a miscellaneous procession of intoxicated students, some of them on horseback. Even if not mounted, though, all were armed with real swords (the bill from Nathans was over £300) and at dinner, as wine flowed, so, in some cases, did tempers rise. Blood was drawn among the guests and a waiter who tried to intervene was lanced in the cheek. My last coherent memory of the evening was the arrival, quite independently, of Lord David Cecil, the newly-appointed Goldsmiths' Professor of English literature, to be told by the manager of the inn: 'We don't want any more of your sort here.'

Forget concours cars, you'll have more fun in a Citroën 2CV

In his first column for Classic Cars *magazine, Alan Clark immediately fires off one of many salvoes attacking American collectors for their ridiculous excess and vanity. Clark is much more interested in driving cars, hates spending money on the way they look and, being a bit of a snob, finds people who are constantly polishing and buffing their machines decidedly bourgeois. Like his art and antiquities, Alan prefers his cars original, slightly scruffy, with an authentic, lived-in look.*

While keeping a car carefully cleaned – particularly the mechanical bits – is fine, over-restoration is anathema to him. But at the same time Alan was conscious of having the correct machinery: Jaguar, Bentley, Porsche and Mercedes were regularly part of his motoring life, but he preferred his cars understated, like his new Bentley Continental S. Alan Clark put a lot of effort into carefully nurturing his cavalier attitude of nonchalance about his fine cars.

In the first three months of this year no fewer than five 8C Alfa Romeos have been sold. Each for over a million pounds. The best one to my mind, i.e. the shabbiest and most original, was bought by Nick Mason – who is probably the most discerning and least show-offy of all the big collectors. Also, he actually drives his cars hard. Driving your car a long distance, like cleaning it very carefully, is the only way to stay in touch.

It's amazing, though, how many 'big' collectors don't do either. The first thing they do to a new acquisition is order a total (meaning gut-its-heart-out) restoration. Then truck it round from one concours to another in an enclosed (and, in the US, air-conditioned) trailer.

If you want to see how far human vanity can go in ruining lovely machinery you should visit the annual show at Pebble Beach – an event so prestigious that multimillionaires who fail to get an award have been known to plead, threaten and weep.

Try, though, to enter something that hasn't had its wheel spokes chromed, or got blue lavatory water in the header tank, and the bouncers will throw you out.

I favour an elimination device. The awards should in the first instance only be provisional. The cars then have to do five laps of the adjacent circuit, flat out, with the entrant at the wheel, before their placing is confirmed.

This is what makes the 8C Alfa so attractive. The engine may let you down, but the handling never will. Rather like the 26C Lago single-seater it has that elusive gift – the ability to change line at any point on a corner without creating a drama.

The 2.9 was faster still but in a curious way had lost charm. They are enormously expensive, of course, so collectors think it is worth spending even more doing them up as the investment is protected.

I sat in a 2.9 Alfa Romeo the other day. It had Farina coachwork, in full '100 point' (always a term of ill-omen) condition. Both vulgar and uncomfortable, with a dreadful driving position.

The only 2.9 that was any good was Hugh Hunter's, which was the fastest car in the famous match race at Brooklands in 1939, set to determine the fastest private sports car. (The race was actually won by a Delahaye 135, but that is another story.) This car was owned for a bit by Tony Crook, the chairman of Bristol Cars, but he could never really get it to run properly and it ended up in Scotland in the collection of Brigadier Thompson.

The Brigadier had a fetish – strange but innocuous. He removed the front wings of every car in his collection and substituted cycle-type mudguards. Sometimes, as in the case of the Alfa, this was regrettable, sometimes as with, for example, a Mercedes-Benz 540K, merely odd. As he was a bachelor, on his death the entire collection was sold at Gleneagles by Sotheby's in 1970, the proceeds going to the Lifeboat Association.

In point of fact, the Association would have been better off putting the whole lot in a shed for a few years, as a beautiful Bentley 8-litre two-seater made £3000 and a Bugatti type 50T, to the astonishment of punters and trade, got as far as £9600.

Nowadays you can move the decimal point to the right – two places, and then some.

But, even in 1996, if you enjoy driving machinery that has character, and are not into male costume jewellery, there are still pleasing things to be found in the £1300–£7000 price band. Early Land-Rovers, obviously. The Station Wagons are more expensive (a relative term, mind) but the canvas 'Tilts' are more fun. If it runs, buy it; anything is curable except rot in the chassis frame and around the spring hangers. And if it's got that bad, then that's probably why the vendor won't allow a demonstration drive . . .

There are lots of good things hidden away under the 'Military Vehicles' heading. Command Cars are out of sight now, at the top end of the price range. But the Dodge Weapon Carrier (same configuration and almost as macho) is great for hurrying in loose urban traffic.

Some of the pick-ups are worth looking at, and Willys Jeeps, like Morris Minors, have a fixed value in the £2000–£3000 range which doesn't seem to alter from year to year.

If you like using up fuel, and staying warm while you do it, the Volvo Sugga 4WD is what estate agents call 'commodious', being based on the pressings of the old Humber Snipe. Two sliding roofs, a fixed map table (with holes for tumblers of schnapps), incredible heater(s) and – a primary quality – it will always start in the mornings. A good one costs £3000.

American cars of the 1940s and early 1950s are a specialized section which deserve a column on their own; but there is real value to be found there, and fun also. Because if you are driving something that doesn't eat money you get such peace of mind; in my 1964 Citroën 2CV I waltz along utterly carefree. The fuel tank always reads full and with one elbow half out of the window flap I am at ease with the world.

The Continental 'R', on the other hand, will overtake anything on the road (except a 911), but in the silence you can hear a distant thrashing noise – the turbulence of world financial markets.

Saltwood

Sunday, 10 September 1978

Back last night after two very pleasant days driving across France. Delicious dinner in clip joint ⋆⋆ restaurant at Arbois. The Chapron went beautifully – being pressed in the last stage at continuous 160–170 kph and running out of petrol, legally, in the Customs shed at Calais.

Then, deterioration: missed seven o'clock boat. Customs kept us waiting an hour and was foiled of a row by being let straight through. Arrived extremely shocked to find George [the jackdaw] had 'gone on Friday'. Greenwood white and grim. Supped on tepid tomato soup and walked into office (11.30 p.m.), masses of useless mail. Livid with James – who was, needless to say, 'out' for the night with the Land-Rover – also I suspect not having nurtured George as he should. Paced about and ate a bit of Nan Howard's (very good) fruit cake and half a mug of hot milk. Slept poorly with Angus taking up most of the room, it seemed.

Morning wet and windy. No sign of George.

Exploding some myths about 'hairy–chested' sports cars

Really obvious and 'showy' sports cars do not appeal to Alan Clark. He can't abide anything Italian and is not impressed by the quintessential sports car, the E-type Jaguar. He's also happy to debunk the idea that big, fast and macho (or hairy-chested) cars are any faster on real roads than well-driven machines, like his wife Jane's Citroën DS23 Decapotable. The Citroën is often quoted as being capable of blowing off more overtly sporting machines and here Clark takes a swipe at Maxwell Beaverbrook for trying so hard in his hairy E-type Jaguar. Hairy-chested sports cars might be heavy on pulling power but most women don't like to travel in them.

What, one might well ask, do we mean by a 'hairy-chested' sports car, anyway? Harsh suspension, scuttle shake, heavy fuel consumption, exhaust noise but – not as common as you might think in these days of turbo lag and/or sharp cam profiles – when you put your foot down, the car gathers speed. Fun to throw about on short (and preferably dry) journeys, too: in other words, 'challenging'.

For the last thirty years, however, the hair has been slowly falling off the chest – or (like mine) going pale grey.

The last truly H-C sports car was the Cadillac-engined J2 Allard. Today, the only thing you can get that's remotely comparable – though so miniaturized and low on the ground that you can count the rivets on the TIR trailer's axle casing as, on locked-up brakes, you dive towards it – is the Caterham. Morgan Plus Eights also demi-qualify. All the other pretend H-C sports cars have been slowly but insidiously ponced. Some even offer electric windows.

Why is this? Partly through design, or sales, department misconceptions about what endows real pulling power (and I'm not referring to torque). Mainly, though, I suggest, it's because H-C cars are ghastly on motorways. They thrum and vibrate both intermittently and unpredictably. Sometimes a gauge will suggest that all is not well. After some hours a smell can be detected – is it hot paint or, worse, just heat? And if the latter, which unlubricated or chafing surface is generating it?

The fuel stops will be frequent, and after filling the tank the starter motor may have to churn the big engine very many times before it belches back into life.

A simple way of shutting out these sensations is, of course, to fold the top down. Ever tried driving the whole way to Gleneagles at 100 mph in an open car? On arrival the tip of your nose will be bright red, the passenger will want to wash her hair at once, and there will be a strange ringing sound in your skull that will persist all through dinner.

Hateful though they are, we all use motorways more and more. So this kind of machinery is doomed, or has limited appeal. All classics have an element of male jewellery about them but H-C sports cars are like chunky costume bracelets.

Their death knell was sounded by the first Audi Quattro. All of a sudden, for those who wanted to get quickly from A to B and enjoy every minute of it, a machine had arrived that flattered the driver and never broke down.

Or, even earlier, one could argue, the Porsche 911 did much the same. It qualifies on every count – speed, agility, excitement (the Great Reaper's wings are audible occasionally, when wet leaves and adverse camber are encountered) – save that of unreliability. In twenty-five years of owning Porsches I have never had one pack up on the road.

In fact you don't have to go that exotic in order to discomfit the hairy-chested ones. A Mercedes 220A with 'export' suspension will give them a lot of hassle (anyone remember a German rally driver called Bohringer?). And on French *routes départementales* I have chased their tails off in my wife's DS23 Decapotable.

In the Citroën I remember overtaking the two Aston Martin

Project 214 cars (you can't get more H-C than that) as they travelled in convoy over the *nids de poules*. Sure they can do 170 mph, or whatever it is, but under these circs they bottomed at more than 90 and emitted orange sparks (God knows what this must have sounded like inside). Later that morning Maxwell Beaverbrook took eight miles to get past us in an E-type coupé so hairy-chested that his wife, Suzy, had to wear ear-defenders throughout the rally.

Interestingly Porsche has toyed, from time to time, with the concept of a blatantly hairy chest – with the early Carreras, of course, and recently the Club Sport. But why bother? The cooking ones will run rings round anything else. Perhaps it is some kind of search for higher sensations, to bring man and machine into closer affinity without the intercession of the servo. And the surest way to do this, in the phrase of America's most redoubtable aircraft designer, is to 'simplicate and add more lightness'.

The nicest-driving classic car ever made is the R-type Bentley Continental, and the result was achieved by applying immensely strict disciplines to the machining of standard components and a rigorous weight-cutting regime at every point in the design stage – even a radio was forbidden on the early A- and B-series.

Now Bentley is trying again – but ignoring the lesson: first cut the weight, ruthlessly, then drive the prototype day and night for six months and see what needs to be put back. In an edition that is deliberately limited by numbers, Bentley should be listening to the enthusiasts, not the sales staff.

To contemplate another field, which will be the truly memorable classic – a shiny new Triumph or a Vincent Shadow of the 1950s with a leather tank muff?

British sports cars are obsolete, so says Alan Clark in 1951!

This article was sent to Mr Kyd at the Motor *magazine on 4 January 1951. Alan hoped that John Aldington of Frazer Nash and Sydney Allard might well reply: 'They usually rise like young salmon to this sort of thing.' Typically he was after getting a vigorous response in the letters pages.*

Alan thought (rightly) that America was a huge potential market but that in about five years' time the Americans might be building their own sports cars, 'unless they are repeatedly convinced that British ones go faster'.

Now, the title to this article is meant not as a direct insult to specialist manufacturers in this country but as a statement of sad fact from which lessons can be learnt. Moreover, before we go any further let me make it quite clear that I am referring only to Allard, Aston-Martin, Frazer Nash and Jaguar, so you boys with Singers and MGs whom nobody ever got past 'cause you make good driving pay and all that, can sit down again because this is about cars that win (or ought to win) races, not classes or 'indexes' or handicaps.

Readers don't need reminding that sports car races on the Continent really are quite something. No one-hour jaunts round aerodrome peri-tracks are they, but a thousand and possibly more miles on genuine roads against experienced and skilful drivers, usually conducting cars that have been built to win just that particular race. To enter an unsuitable car for these events is all very fine and English and so on but it does the country of origin and the manufacturer very little good indeed because, unlike certain British motor journalists, the Continentals do not consider that just to finish a race constitutes 'a jolly good show'.

Confusion as to suitability may be partly attributed to differences of nomenclature in the various countries, for example; many English 'sporty cars' are very far removed from the Continental idea of a *voiture de grand sport*. So let us quickly resubdivide cars into three categories. At the bottom we have the small underpowered draughty little things that will none of them exceed 80 [mph] and are built for people who (apparently) don't like going fast but think they can drive like hell. There are so many of these people that they constitute a class and they will race happily with one another. These cars, which we may call quasi-sports cars, have one advantage: they are cheap. Not so cheap as all that, however, for many examples of the next class come cheaper.

This next class we may call fast tourers. Taking the price limit as around £1000 in the free markets of the world, it is dominated by the Jaguars XK and Mark VII and the Cadillac convertible. There are a lot of good fast comfortable cars in this section: Oldsmobile, Nash, Ford, are all names that spring to mind. I think it a great pity that the mass of readers in England are precluded from enjoying the pleasures of these excellent vehicles at first hand. To those who maintain that they don't corner I would reply that it is simply a matter of GVTS and a heavy right foot. If you don't believe me ask anyone who saw an Olds 88 win the Variety Class of the Coupe du Monde at Spa, against other vehicles whose names had best remain under a cloud.

Finally there is the top class, with which this article is concerned. Here the sky is the limit as far as price is concerned and every member is a potential race winner; these are the real *voitures de grand sport*. Ferrari is king, with those very genuine* sports cars like the Mons Talbots, a close second. I'm afraid the English contingent are lurking coyly in the shadows of this section, but at least two could emerge into the limelight if they did the right things.

* You're right, my tongue *is* in my cheek.

Let us consider the less hopeful cases first. Frazer Nash is an excellent example of a very good design developed to the limit. The old 328 BMW was one of the great sports cars, but that design is now thirteen years old, and however intelligently modified, painstakingly constructed and ably driven, that car is no longer going to win races outright. It may win its class on occasions when the Ferraris blow one another up, and I suppose it might have pulled off Le Mans in 1949. But 'might' is not 'did' and 1949 was certainly very different from what 1951 looks like being. So someone might take Aldington on one side and whisper that what he needs is not a new engine or a new chassis but a new car. (If he wants his products to win races.)

Next there is the Allard. We have only to consider one model and that is the J2 with Cadillac motor. This car was third at Le Mans in 1950, and if it had had a Cadillac gearbox, it might have done even better, but I have a hunch that that was its high water mark. The Cadillac is a wonderful motor with 92 square inches of piston area, but there's only one other good thing about the 32 and that's the Dedion rear axle. The weight distribution and the front suspension still possess a distinct streak of their trials-bred forebears, which is just no good at all for real road racing, two miles a minute being very different from life in a mud pit. Nonetheless, the Cadillac 32 is a cinch for any round-the-houses race and is a sensational performer, giving a distinct thrill when you pump your foot in bottom. Moreover this car is cock o' the roost in the US where, naturally, the art of tuning domestic engines is very highly developed and where owners of more or equally potent machinery possibly find them more difficult to conduct than the three-speed, swing-axle J2.

Mention of the US is an appropriate moment to consider the prospects of Jaguar for there are more XK120s in North America than in the whole of the rest of the world put together. Moreover, whereas the exploits of the XKs in Europe do great good to the prestige of the country and the motor industry as a whole, they are of little direct relevance to the factory's order books since with the exception of the Swiss and the Belgians, European currency is wretchedly soft. But in the US it is I think vital that these cars should compete successfully. You see, the XK is bought mainly by playboys, movie stars and general flashabouts.* These boys usually have very little idea of how to drive and get badly beaten if they ever try their hand at racing. But half the reason they bought one in the first place was because it was the fastest car in the world and couldn't be beaten by anything. This reputation has got to be maintained. It would pay the factory if two good English drivers with properly prepared cars competed in the major American events this year. And properly prepared cars means something very different from the XK as it emerges from the factory (I am the proud and happy owner of one in this state). Remember, in the US, at any rate, it does not matter whether the car looks different: if the name wins the race, the production is sold.

Let us consider, then, what would have to be done to these cars to give them a chance at Le Mans this year, because that is the most gruelling test of all, and any car that wins at Sarthe will clean up all the little Hanley Tank meetings in the States. Leslie Johnson nearly pulled it off at Le Mans in 1950 but this year [1951] it is going to be very different and those cars have got to sweat off a lot of weight before they go into the ring again. Pause for a minute and survey the opposition: there are our old friends the Lago Talbots; there are at least two V12 4½ litre Ferrari saloons and innumerable Ferraris of intermediate litreage; one and possibly two OSCA V12s also of 4½ litres; a rumoured 4½ [litre] Mercedes; not to mention the usual crop of Simcas and Delahayes and the boys from God's own country, sexy as the devil in their special Cadillacs. I think Jaguars, conducted by Moss and Johnson, could still do it, but they must shed at least 1000 lb and go to town under the prototype ruling with rapier-slim, light-alloy bodies, spoke wheels and plenty of cooling air wafting over the brake drums. I know several people in the States who would pay double the price of an ordinary XK for a Le Mans replica on those lines and it might pay the factory to introduce as a 'one-off' model built to order. Certainly it would be worse than useless to commit this delightful touring car to

* Real enthusiasts who buy an XK for pleasure usually *compete* in something else.

The first motoring photograph to capture an image of Alan Clark behind the wheel. He is seventeen and the car is his 2½-litre Jaguar SS 100. Actually his second car, it replaced a Vintage Bentley 6½-litre, which he had bought in the summer of 1946 while still a pupil at Eton. The black Jaguar has a white border painted around its perimeter, a hangover from the 'blackout' during World War II when cars were driven with minimal lighting. Piloting the car home to Hampstead for the first time Alan managed to spin it. Surviving the mishap he went on to drive it to the Isle of Skye in Scotland in an uninterrupted eighteen-hour stint, then around a good deal of Czechoslovakia as well as to Sintra in Portugal. Alan Clark was an intrepid motorist from the off!

His beloved Jaguar XK120 which was bought new in November 1950 from City Motors in Oxford, where Alan was an undergraduate. The new Jaguar would be his calling card, roaring up the King's Road in the XK doing his boy-racer stuff. Later, in the early Fifties, he lived for a time in Monte Carlo where he attached himself to a ballet company (for personal reasons) … carving around the streets at all hours with three and sometimes four dancers squeezed into the front seat. He never sold the XK and thought he must be the only person 'with his own hair and teeth' who still owned an XK120 he had bought new.

From top to bottom

The Volkswagen Beetle pictured with Jane in 1958, the year they married. Alan was competing in the hill-climb at Firle in Sussex, which he won. Jane is wearing a pair of earrings Alan had just given her. The unsuspecting Beetle has had its hubcaps remove and is about to be thrashed up the hill. Years later the humble little Volkswagen w seriously uprated when Ala shoe-horned a Porsche 356 engine under its rear lid turning it into an effective giant-killer.

Alan never liked Italian car much, thinking Ferraris in particular were for poseurs, very rarely actually driven by their owners. There wer a few exceptions though, including the 275GTB4, the 340MM and the 750 Monza. Here, sometime in the Fifties, Alan is enjoying a Monza on the Abetone pass with the Ferrari works driver, Sighinolfi. He found the Ferrari driver to be 'cruel, unfeeling, needlessly impatient in breaking his steed'. Later he read that the same car crashed on the Abetone killing the uncour Sighinolfi.

An early snap of Jane and son James with the Ford coupé. This is a similar American car to the Buick in which Alan lost his licence while at Oxford. H committed the 'relatively trivial offence' of having a on his lap – she was doing steering while he operated the foot pedals from benea her. A dextrous fellow.

Another American car, this time a pale blue Fifties Oldsmobile which appears to have a British Automobile Racing Club badge mounted on the front bumper. Alan loved early American cars because they were so solidly built and had lusty great engines. He felt they were underrated in Britain.

The Mercedes 600 on one of the many trips to the chalet in Zermatt, Switzerland. James, Andrew and Jane (in the front seat) are pictured with their governess. The car was sold forthwith after breaking down with fuel-injection problems in Spain in 1973, stranding the young family in the middle of rush-hour traffic with not a word of Spanish between them. So much for Mercedes-Benz reliability!

Judging by the yellow trouser suit and Ford Cortina in the background this snap was taken in the late Sixties with Alan competing once again, this time in the Jaguar XK120. The car has its full-width windscreen fitted, although sometimes he ran it with the smaller aero-screens. The car had benefited from upgrades by Jaguar competitions boss 'Lofty' England including the removal of the rear spats, the fitting of wire wheels and improved brakes along with a C-type cylinder head and other engine modifications. After all this work Alan later admitted to preferring the car in its original specification.

From top to bottom

The Citroën 2CV, or 'the Mickey' as it was affectionately known, somewhere in the Alps near Zermatt. Alan piled the whole family into the little car and drove it from England all the way to Switzerland. He always drove it flat out. With very little power the momentum had to be maintained so he cornered it on the door handles, particularly around London. On one occasion in the 2CV, as he related in his *Diaries*, the police pulled him over for speeding. Being breathalised he viewed as 'amusement'. Fortunately he was completely sober.

A Willys Jeep bought when the Clarks lived in Devon in the Sixties. Here it is on the estate in Eriboll, Scotland with Alan, James and his wife Julie. Although Alan liked Land-Rovers and this Jeep, he was outraged to learn that a similar one had won the 1997 Peking-Paris rally. 'No one drives a Jeep for more than sixty miles for pleasure.' He regarded the Peking-Paris epic as 11,000 miles of purgatory in such a machine, but would have loved to have competed in one of his American cars.

The Austin Seven saloon known as Ruby was bought with the intention of being done up so Jane could use it to trundle down to Hythe from Saltwood. Alan could not resist it because it was in totally original condition. James got it running at one point, but nothing much else has happened since then.

This fearsome 1947 Talbot Lago single-seater racing car was the number one car in the French team, driven to victory by Louis Chiron in the French Grand Prix of 1949. Doug Whiteford twice won the Australia Grand Prix with it. Alan never raced the Talbot but Jane's brother, Mike Beuttler, a Formula 1 and Formula 3 driver, campaigned it for a time until it had to be sold in the early Seventies to raise some much-needed cash. 'Until you have driven a Talbot Lago your motoring experience is incomplete,' noted Alan.

Right For some strange reason Alan had two 1967 Chevrolet Impalas in his fleet. The hard-top pictured here was known as the 'winter car' and a near-identical soft-top was known as the 'summer car'. Both proved totally reliable and were very well made. They always passed their MoT tests, but were mainly used for pottering around Salt-wood and consequently have done very little mileage.

Below Victory day at Silverstone Circuit, April 1969. The big Mercedes 600 is parked next to the 'Bira' Bentley. This very early 1934 Vanden Plas-bodied 3½-litre Derby Bentley was once the property of H. H. Prince Chakrabougse of Siam. Better known as Prince Bira, the playboy racing driver loved this Silent Sport Car and regularly drove it non-stop with Prince Chula to Monte Carlo and Biarritz. Alan kept the 'Bira' in original, scruffy condition, retaining its well-worn interior, thus preserving the car's nostalgic link with the elegant days of its flamboyant past.

Alan Clark in action driving his first 1923 Rolls-Royce Silver Ghost in the
1973 Great Alpine Rally, organised by the Rolls-Royce Enthusiasts' Club as
a commemoration of the original Alpine Rally first run in 1913.

Here the Silver Ghost is at rest in a car park. The car was rebodied with this
light skiff- or boat-tail bodywork. Alan had the engine's performance improved
by fitting two carburettors and upping the compression ratio. It was know as the
'bi-carb' but was sold and later replaced with another Ghost with more drastic,
minimalist bodywork.

Two Derby Bentleys, cars which Alan really appreciated, because they are so beautifully made, offer very good performance and are very low-key. The scruffy car on the left, the 'Barnato', was reputedly owned by Woolf Barnato, another playboy and Bentley racing driver of the Twenties and Thirties, one of the infamous 'Bentley Boys'. The car on the right has the desirable open Vanden Plas tourer coachwork. Alan believed the early 4¼-litre Derbys built in 1936 are the most desirable – they were the fastest cars Bentley built before the war. He liked the fact because it gets up the nose of the tweedy whiskers brigade who opine the only Bentleys worth having (old boy) are the pre-war vintage models, the ones referred to by Ettorio Bugatti as fast lorries. Alan researched the figures and, sure enough, Derbys are quicker.

A line-up of Bentley Continentals at Saltwood. These are unique cars: on the left is the 1958 S1 Continental which has the rare manual transmission and power steering, one of only three ever built in this specification; in the centre, the 1953 R-type Continental; on the right, the 1954 R-type Continental Special. This is the only Continental to have been rebodied. It was stolen in the Sixties and overturned in the New Forest, killing the thief and two unfortunate hitch-hikers. The bodywork was severely damaged and Alan bought the write-off and had Bentley specialist, Bradley Brothers, discard the damaged skin, shorten the chassis and fit the Special bodywork.

From top to bottom

Having covered only 23,000 miles from new, once the property of H. H. the Maharajah of Jaipur, this 1937 Rolls-Royce Phantom III proved irresistible. The Sedanca coachwork by Barker has rather flash Art Nouveau finishings. As James Clark remembers, the Rolls arrived in a crate directly from Bombay docks. When the container was opened all sorts of insects and spiders ran out followed by a glorious waft of the exotic East. The subsequent stench of stale petrol, though, was a realistic spoiler.

The original 'John Player Special', this 1937 Rolls-Royce 25/30 was bought new by John Player and remained in his possession until Alan bought it in 1970. Despite its conservative design, the Weymann fabric saloon was unexpectedly light and great fun to drive. Alan loved its originality being, 'one owner, chauffeur-maintained, complete service record from new'. This is what a Rolls-Royce felt like in its prime.

A very fit-looking Alan with his Rolls-Royce Silver Shadow, not the sort of car you would expect Alan to want. Correct, he bought it solely for the number plate – AC 1800.

another year of being flogged round road circuits without serious modification.

Finally there is the Aston Martin. Here surely is an example of a very good car arriving exactly a year late. There should have been a team one, two, threeing, in 1949 instead of one car retiring with the sort of fault that ought to have been discovered in the first weeks of road testing. Now of course that good little engine is much too small; but it occurs to one that there is a solution. Under the same roof at Kelham is the power unit that will make the DB II 90. In 1939 V12 Lagondas were third and fourth at the very reputable speed of 84 mph, on a circuit that was considerably slower than it is today and were pulling heavy and unsuitable chassis. Put this engine in the current AM saloon★ and you have a fastish car − 'Won't fit?' Heavens above, man, a competent staff of German mechanics could install it inside twelve hours. I know it's an old design but it would make the car go fast enough to rattle the Wogs† this year while the AM experimental department banked the two WO Bentley sixes together. It might even win a race, and seriously, unless something is done, I don't think British cars will win one Continental or American sports car race in 1951.

Jaguar clearly took note. The C-type won Le Mans in 1951 and 1953. − Robert Coucher

★ Substitute Lockheeds for the present brakes.
† AC was writing in 1951.

Selecting four 'as new' fantasy cars – no price would be too high

Alan does not think that old cars can really be made as new because there will always be some component that acts its age. But given the choice, he selects four cars he knows and loves. Typically, though, he ends with an oddball, one of his favourite machines – the scruffy Beetle fitted with a Porsche 356 engine.

This is a good example of a Q-car: a normally staid-looking machine with a more powerful engine and uprated suspension. The term Q-car comes from Q-boats, which were merchant vessels manned by the Royal Navy during the last war with hidden guns used to deceive and destroy submarines. Real drivers love Q-Cars because they can be used to great effect in the cut-and-thrust of fast driving, surprising those jumped-up drivers in their ostensibly faster machines. There's nothing like a good motoring put-down, is there?

I have always believed that no matter what you do by way of renovation or replacement, you can never really make worn–out machinery 'as good as new'.

I suppose if every single component, from camshaft to dipswitch, is unwrapped mint or machined from the solid, you ought to get close – assuming parity of assembly techniques – but are they ever? There is always something, from the block (the water passages, whatever you do, will never be as free as they should) to the bearings on reverse gear that are 'good for another 100,000 miles'.

I must admit I have never driven a Vicarage Mark II, or one of those 'new' XK140s made by Vitesse Engineering. And apparently, *true* replica Ferrari 250GTOs are being built in a tiny airtight clinic in Japan. (But as an inscrutable silence has pervaded this project for over a year, they may have hit problems.)

So my preference, longing you could say, is for very low-mileage examples. Indeed, as a card-carrying nostalgicist I find it very hard to resist *anything* (except a 1960s Standard 8 or a Reliant) if it has plainly done less than 10,000 miles.

An instructive fantasy is to select the four cars you would most like to take delivery of new – this weekend.

My own list doesn't change much. First, a 1908 Ghost with 'sprinting gear', a very light body and basket-weave seats like a Sopwith Camel.

Next, the limited-edition Mercedes SSKL that was made for Rudi Caracciola, in which he won the 1931 Mille Miglia, Hans Stuck and others. (Interesting, wasn't it, that when the Swiss closed off the Klausen hill climb last year and allowed a lot of very rich people to make timed runs in their exotic Alfas, GP single-seaters and so on, no one managed to beat Caracciola's record for the old dirt and *pavé* surface.)

Third, a 1952 Bentley R-type Continental. My own example I really love. It is not new, and never can be made so. Yet it is still such a good car that I often wonder what they were like when driven out of Jack Barclay's showroom for the first time.

Fourth – and some may find this humble choice surprising – is the Porsche 356B, the *Damen* model, being the 'softest' of the three engine options.

I seem to have spent most of my thirties in 356s. Everywhere they took me: Italy, Switzerland, Greece, Crete, Ischia, France. Never went wrong, never even rattled. I did enormous mileages and then sold them, thinking that I could always find a nearly new one to carry on with until, one day, the supply dried up.

The fastest was a Super, which would actually go round into the red in top at 120 mph. The least pleasant was a Super '90', whose 'developed' engine was by then getting a little bit harsh. All-time favourite was the last, a *Damen* convertible bought second-hand (or pre-owned as one now must say) which I drove and drove until it almost literally fell to pieces with rust; and all I have left is the hood frame, the bumpers and the instruments, plus see below.

That car was completely unburstable, and never did less than 28 mpg, often nearer 40. Yes, on a wet road, an adverse camber or in a high wind, you had to be *circumspect*. If all three of these phenomena coincided it might have been better to abandon the Porsche altogether and drive something with its own governor, like an early Land-Rover.

But this is simply genetics, because the Porsche 356 is no more than a refined, lowered, widened, beautifully made Beetle. For real thrills, do an engine swap – it goes straight in and takes about four hours – and only use it on wet days!

When I broke my 356 convertible I put the engine into our 1956 school-run Beetle, prudently also saving and fitting the big, horizontally finned brake drums and drilled wheels. Coyly, the rev counter now sits beside the standard 80 mph speedo. Otherwise there is no indication whatever that this shabby, somewhat scarred and crumpled £300 medical student's ancillary is going to outdrag the rep's Cavalier when the lights go green.

Under some circs the Beetle will actually handle better than a 356. The key modification is to have Michelin X tyres inflated to 28 lb at the rear, normal cross-plies at 26 lb on the front.

Perhaps it is the driving position, or the more direct steering, but it is often possible to set up the VW in a drift with all four wheels pointing in the same direction; while the recommended technique for the Porsche – of *wischen*, or 'wiping' the tail – can, in my experience at least, lead all too suddenly to wiping *out*.

The one sad thing is that it is practically impossible to get the engines rebuilt. They were real little jewels of precision; but the factory won't supply exchange units any longer and most branches of Bash & Fixit simply aren't up to it.

Which brings me back to my original point. There are some things for which, if today one could find them new, no price would be too high.

Chain-driven Edwardian monsters can still send thrills and chills down a driver's spine

Alan loves mechanical simplicity, where the machine offers the driver plenty of unfettered feel. He has completed a number of epic journeys in his Rolls-Royce Silver Ghost including two Alpine rallies, which consist of thousands of miles up and down the Alps. He is less sure about his 1910 chain-driven Locomobile but it remains 'heroic' to drive.

The chain-driven Frazer Nashes and Rolls-Royce Silver Ghosts are about as far apart, in tactile terms, as any two marques on the Vintage car scene. In one you sit in a kind of canvas torpedo tube where a sneeze is all the driver needs to get round a ninety-degree corner and a paper bag in the street can be felt through the 'suspension'. In a Ghost you are high, high above the traffic; being drawn along, as has often been said, by a piece of string; this car's long wheelbase and cantilever springs gave it a ride better than anything else until the ID Citroëns arrived.

But what these two have in common is that they – and they alone, it seems, among pre-war machinery – are capable of journeying to the Alps and coping with day-in, day-out pass-storming rallies. I ran my own car in the 1993 Alpine Commemorative – nearly three weeks on the Alps; the equivalent of climbing Mount Everest five times. It is so light, with its skimpy military pick-up body, that it could run much faster times than the more formal cars. But I do remember one hot afternoon on the Brocon pass – a 40 per cent grade – when it stopped. It didn't hiss (the steam had all gone long ago); it just ticked, menacingly. No matter, I filled it up with water from a stream nearby, put in a quart of oil for luck, selected reverse gear, turned on the magneto and let the clutch out. It started in its own length and never played that trick again.

Of course 'Nashes will run rings round any Rolls in the mountains. They, too, are tough; capable of functioning still when – Sayings of the Royal Air Force No. 6 – there is 'nothing on the clock but the maker's name'; or, worse, when the needle has crept right round to start again at the 'S' of Smiths Industries. But somewhere along the 'Nash trail there always seems to be somebody with their car jacked up on the verge, apparently washing (?) the chain in an enamel basin of paraffin. Or perhaps they're changing a link?

My own experience with 'Nashes is very limited – between starting off confidently, the first corner and the mini-incident that then occurred. But it was enough to realize that these are wonderful, mystic living creatures – with teeth.

Regular readers will know that I am trying always to circumvent the servo or 'power-assist'; that I prefer mechanical linkages to hydraulic ones or (worst of all) 'printed circuits'. And, of all devices, the chain works like this in the transmission.

I think that among all the machinery I have ever conducted the most frightening (and is not fear part of the flavour of experience?) was an HRD 1000 cc Black Shadow. There was nothing else, until the advent of the Bentley Continental 'R', where one seemed always to have an actual speed 20 mph above one's visual estimate. On an old bike, which you have to set up some way off from the corner, this could mean 'Hullo, there!' on the grass verge on the other side. But with big cylinders, and light frames, and high cogs, you can really feel movement.

Very occasionally I take out a 1910 chain-drive Locomobile. It ran in the Vanderbilt Cup of 1911 and finished fourth, then it was up-engined with a Wisconsin T-head of 11 litres (very Peter Helck). I can't say that driving it on the road is pleasant but it sure is heroic. The brakes are about as good as those of a Raleigh pushbike and, as it will exceed 70 mph across Romney Marsh, I have sometimes contemplated fitting a teeny drogue parachute that might slow me down before I arrive in Rye. It does make you realize, though, that the Paris–Madrid road race – all Edwardian chain-drive monsters, and which had to be stopped halfway because so many people had been killed – would have made the Imola Grand Prix seem like your local kart track.

After 'Babs' cut its driver in half at 170 mph chains went out of fashion. But with today's high-tensile steels and computer design they can be as resilient as any shaft. If you go to Silverstone for a Vintage meeting you will see that the tiny Morgan three-wheelers now have little difficulty in cutting up all those Massey-Fergusons with round radiators and a 'B' emblem on the front.

I often wonder why there is not a greater proliferation of that great scare-trap of the 1920s – the Shelsley Special. There is a growing club of enthusiasts making, or devising, aero-engined specials, using Liberty or Maybach colossi. But these are not genuine Edwardian cars. They have no history or myth. If it is sensation that you seek, the same effect – cubed – is waiting from any good Japanese bike engine, and transmission, in the kind of 'chassis' that John Bolster used in Bloody Mary; or, more advanced, the Fry brothers with the Freikaiserwagen.

There is 300 bhp per ton waiting here. I suppose there might be problems with the Construction and Use legislation, though – unless, of course, you were able to get it through under the new regulations for taxing powered skateboards.

Jaguars are the favourite Clark marque

Alan thought his beloved Jaguar XK120 one of the most enjoyable cars he ever owned. He also loved his C-type, had a brief flirtation with a D-type, enjoyed an XK140 coupé for years, but found his red E-type horrid with its disconcerting independent rear suspension.

This issue has such good and compelling Jaguar material that I find myself stuck in Memory Lane. I took delivery of a new Jaguar XK120 in November 1950. And it is still here in the garage. I doubt if there are many people who still own a car they bought forty-six years ago. And I would bet money that in no case is the car an XK120.

To this day I can recall the amazement at this absolute quantum leap in sports-car design. Yes, the BMW 328 had gone halfway just before the war. But the XK was so soft and silky: the power just went on and on pouring out. Engine speed was redlined at least 1000 rpm higher than any other 'performance' car – yet it was so comfortable, so free of vibration, flat spots, fussy torque curve. A party trick was to do a standing start against a 2½ litre (Riley-engined) Elliot-Healey belonging to a friend – at that time billed as the 'fastest four-seater car in the world', a works entry having done well in the 1949 Mille Miglia.

The Jaguar was only allowed to use top gear. A bit of juddering and hot smell at the outset, but invariably the XK120 caught the Healey before they were through 100 mph ... and then, of course, disappeared into the distance.

Peter Blond, who used to run the car division at Sotheby's, was a schoolmate of mine. And, as a couple of bumptious seventeen-year-olds we thought we could handle anything in our SS100s. Peter was a much harder driver than I and went on, of course, to drive C-, D-type and Lister Jaguars very effectively in the early 1960s. I lost count of the number of times he blew up the engine of his SS on the A5 – usually on that fast three-lane bit north of Dunstable. So when I first appeared in the XK and offered him a start he laughed. But it was no contest, of course.

Because that was the competition. T-type MGs? T stands for tinky. 'Aerodynamic' HRGs? A joke. Lea-Francis? A boring joke. Allard? Slower than the XK in third. Austin Atlantic? Slow, and with 'hydro-mechanical' brakes – which meant only the front shoes ever came into contact with the drums. There was also a strange, whale-like Alvis two-seater and, to my mind, nicest of the alternatives, the first 4 litre Jensens.

The XK in its early form, with small-bore SUs, 7:1 comp ratio and dual exhausts was amazingly fast in a straight line, and would go into the red even on the 3.27 axle ratio; aerodynamics helped by spats and undershield. I recall getting the needle round all the way at night on the Witney bypass (good going in 1951) and, the following year, reaching 218 kph on the Le Mans circuit.

Only Stirling Moss had the genius to make it perform 'straight out of the showroom' – his 1950 TT win in a borrowed car at the age of twenty made the XK seem more formidable than it really was. Biondetti, who won the Mille Miglia more often than any other driver, told Jaguar: 'This is a road car: reduce the weight by 300 kg and put that incredible engine in a short, tubular-frame chassis.' Thus was born the C-type.

There was an awful lot of snobbery about Jaguars in those days. To many they were still redolent of Wardour Street, camel-hair coats and cheap cigars. In my last year at Oxford, Patrick Lindsay and John Ormsby-Gore brought a 2.3 8C Alfa to show the XK – which I'd been showing off for months – the quick way round the block.

It didn't work. The Alfa was tired and smoky and, as it was not worth much, few knew how to keep it in tune. Once again the XK triumphed and the 8C degenerated into a static metal hunk. You could have bought it off them for £400.

In 1953 the faithful 120 went back to the factory to be prepared for the Carrera Panamericana. Heavy suspension, a sixty-gallon tank, close-ratio 'box (only introduced on the works C-types that summer), 9:1 compression and 2 in. SUs. The beautiful lines were broken by discarding the spats and fitting wire wheels and (Dunlop) disc brakes.

I suppose it was faster. It certainly felt harder and noisier. But tiny babies soon began to make their appearance, and I found myself using the XK less and less. I became infatuated with a series of saloons: the 3.4 Mark I (that really was a car; it didn't have any brakes at all), the 3.8 Mark II, and lastly the Coombs 3.8.

'Alan,' a friend said after a short demo, 'you have finally found the car in which you are going to get killed.' I kept the Coombs for a long while, until the doors began to shimmy at high speeds; then I remembered his warning and parted with it.

The great thing about the twin-cam Jaguar is that in any configuration it can be made to go well, and in some hands it is – in road terms at least – still truly competitive. An extraordinary accomplishment for a design nearly fifty years old.

X marks the spot: a personal appreciation of the Jaguar XK

An early piece written in 1951, this is a perceptive and accurate view of actually owning a Jaguar XK120 when new. Here Alan concludes that the Jaguar has given him more pleasure than any other car. The fact that he kept it all his life supports the opinion he formed in the early 1950s: that the Jaguar XK120 was one of the best ever...

I know that it is always tiresome to read an article by a private owner about some interesting car in his possession and to find that it consists entirely of praise and loud boasting, so I will accordingly endeavour to modulate the former and refrain entirely from the latter.

A great deal of nonsense has been, and in some quarters still is, talked about the XK. When it was first announced, many cried that it could not possibly be put on the market at the ridiculously low price of £988, and that only a few record-breaking cars could be built for advertisement. Others went to the other extreme and proclaimed that, since the car covered more of the Silverstone circuit in the 1949 Production Car race than three of the ERAs competing in the Grand Prix, it was an immediate certainty for Le Mans and the Mille Miglia.

Later it was easy, by compounding a synthesis of these two propositions, for the sour-grapers to maintain that since XKs were being built at the rate of forty a day, costs must be being kept down somehow (sinister inference) and anyhow look at the way they were being licked by Allards and Talbots, which just proved it. Indeed, I confess to holding the first view myself; my reaction when the car was first displayed at Earls Court was, like that of every other enthusiast: it simply *can't* be true.

Now what exactly is '*it*'? I maintain that it is simply a very fast and utterly reliable two-seater tourer with high comfort and safety factors. In my opinion – though I admit that Leslie Johnson and others have gone towards proving this wrong – the XK as it emerges from Coventry is *not* a suitable competition sports car. Not, that is to say, suitable for sports car competition in the highly developed Continental sense of the term. But do not the majority of us buy our car for competition not on some foreign track but on the open road where conditions are less arduous and victory can be just as sweet? How many readers share the admittedly heretical view of a Californian friend of mine? At Earls Court this year we were at the stand of a British sports car firm which charges twice as much as Jaguar for a car that is 10 mph slower, and we became involved in an argument over the merits of the rival products. Our opponent fired what he hoped was a final shaft. 'It depends,' he remarked with dignity, 'on what you want in a car.'

'Hell, man!' replied my companion. 'I buy a sports car for just two things – trapping dolls and passing Cadillacs.'

And I hope I'm not treading on anyone's toes when I say that I think that it was with those objects in mind that the XK was originally conceived and that it achieves them with supreme ability. But to say this is to put the XK's merits at their lowest, and in fact as we all know it is not only the most beautiful-looking and the fastest car ever made in England, but an absolutely standard version can win an Alpine rally.

One of the most pleasurable features of the XK is the practical and aesthetic excellence of the cockpit. The abundance of leather, trim and firm, the cleverly designed steering wheel with the golden Jaguar head in the boss, and the expensive-looking and accurate Smiths instruments give the passenger and driver a delicious anticipation of quality which is in no wise dispelled by the car's performance. Not that the XK does not feel almost ordinary when one first gets in and proceeds in cautious fashion through the gears, and even when she gets a little bolder it is difficult to appreciate her performance without constant glances at the speedometer or direct comparison with other vehicles.

There is none of the, literally, breathtaking surge of a Cadillac-Allard or a hot-rod and when one demands maximum acceleration from bottom or low revs in second, one is conscious of the 28-odd hundredweight attached to the prop shaft. But at about 50 [mph] in second with the engine running between 4000 and 5000 rpm and with over 1000 revs still in hand, the feeling of exultation is tremendous. That driver of a Cadillac (or anything else for that matter) who had a nasty gleam in his eye at the last traffic light looks as if he had selected reverse by mistake. The extraordinarily intoxicating thing about the XK acceleration is that it feels *progressive*. To express it in the simplest Russell and Whitehead language, she seems to be going (faster) and (faster) [faster and faster]. That this is no proud owner's illusion can be ascertained by a quick check with the *Autocar* road test figures, which show the car to be quicker from 70 to 80 mph than from 60 to 70.

To slow up this beautifully dressed and very unobtrusive demon king of the road, one has a highly efficient set of Lockheeds, which give 207 square inches of lining area. Very efficient, that is, in ordinary weather, but when there is a lot of water about, one's rate and direction of deceleration become less predictable. To prevent the entry of water, Jaguar now provide baffle plates which should, in wintertime, be worn over the air scoops of the front drums, but my own experience is that in severe conditions the water still manages to penetrate.

The steering is quite delightful, light at all speeds, accurate and totally oblivious to road shocks. It is not unduly high geared but sufficiently sensitive to allow the car to 'correct its own sides'. The lock is excellent and one can make a U-turn in most main streets.

Some of the first cars delivered in the States had a rather poor body finish and I noticed some very shabby ones over there last spring [1950], but I am assured by the production manager of Jaguar that current cars have eight coats of paint baked on to them, and certainly my own car shows no sign of losing its complexion. One or two early coachwork rattles have been cured and the whole body now feels as tight as a drum.

Criticisms? Very difficult to find any. I dislocated my wrist trying to change down from top to third while running the car in, but the gearbox is now very pleasant to feel. The hood, too, took some mastering; blood was drawn, and the horn used to get jammed on, via the medium of the tip-forward seats, when heavy showers overtook one outside maternity hospitals. My only serious criticism is that driver visibility with the hood up is rather poor, particularly at night, due to the shallow angle of the windscreen, and the fact that the excellently constructed side screens tend to get rather opaque.

But with the Basic Things of the car I can find no fault. The engine is truly magnificent in appearance and performance and is, I think, the finest internal combustion engine ever produced in this country. It is absolutely reliable, has no suggestion of a flat spot, feels as if it will run up to 8000 rpm, is mechanically incredible, will not pink or run on, uses no oil or water and gives gas mileages as high as 32 mpg (normal dicing around gives 22).

Performance? My car seems, if anything, faster than those used by the press to which data I would refer readers. Point to Point Averages are always astonishing even if they represent hundreds of miles without ever shifting from high (don't forget that top gear acceleration from 20 to 40 mph, identical to M. Dynaflow Brick) and one can always be certain of looking at one's watch and finding it earlier than one had thought.

In conclusion I should like to say that no car I have ever owned has given me so much pleasure and that every time I drive it, still, I always get the feeling that it ought to have cost around £2000.

Modern cars, no matter how fast, don't offer thrills the way classics do

Alan rightly concedes that modern cars are now so fast and capable that you really need to be doing very silly speeds to enjoy, or even experience, the sensation of speed. He is also a little annoyed that apparently ordinary saloon cars are now so capable. In the past an E-type was in a different league to the ordinary cars that it shared road space with. That gap has all but disappeared today, even with a Porsche 911 and Bentley Continental 'S'.

Speed, speed, glorious speed ... No other sensation (or only one) compares. It is in the nature of all warm-blooded creatures to enjoy movement; dogs and children, content if not somnolent while a car is moving, get fretful and fidgety when it's still. But it's when one starts to taste the spice of danger that it becomes intoxicating.

Now it has first to be said that speed kills. Broadly, the higher the speed, the lower the chances of survival if things go wrong. One of the most disagreeable features of VHSAs (Very High Speed Accidents) is that they go on and on for such a long time. The giant, molten skidmark; the spin; the shunt; the sideswipe; the somersault; the roll ... If you are doing over 120 mph when things go wrong you can suffer all of these in succession while praying that friction and fracture don't bring about ignition. I remember Peter Riley, who suffered a bad spinal injury in the 1962 Liège–Rome–Liège event when his Austin-Healey 3000 went through a *lacet* halfway down the Stelvio, saying that the really nasty bits were the *silences*, when the vehicle was in the air.

None of this, which is inseparable from laws of physics that govern the dispersal of kinetic energy, has altered. But suspension design, soundproofing, insulation from tactile warning, have had the effect of lifting the *apparent* threshold. You can be more easily and acutely frightened skiing at 35 mph in icy ruts than driving at three times that speed in a Silver Shadow when a TIR lorry changes lanes in front of you.

To get the thrill of speed today you can go back in time. Try a fifty-year-old Triumph Tiger too. But in a modern car you need to be driving at a speed where anticipation of crisis demands so high a level of concentration that the sensation is barely enjoyable. This is what makes me pessimistic for the XK8 (and all other contemporary 'sports' cars, come to that). What's the point? Killjoys used to say, 'Where can you use the performance?' (to which the correct answer is, 'Just leave that bit to me'). Now there is a choice of a dozen four-door sedans that will exceed 130 mph, the speed at which you have to start straining your eyes towards the traffic agglomeration after next. Some, like the Audi A8 and performance variants of the C-class Mercedes, are more secure than and, in practical terms, just as fast as the 'hyper' two-seaters.

When the E-type arrived thirty-five years ago it had a colossal margin – nearly 60 mph – over practically anything else on the road. The fact that the car, particularly in roadster configuration, was absolutely vile, with strange rear-wheel steering (not unlike a Range Rover on a badly cambered motorway) at more than 120, did not matter. No one needed to 'explore the envelope'. Everything else vanished from the driving mirror.

Nowadays I drive two very fast cars – a 911 and a Bentley Continental 'S'. Most of the time they will get past cheaper stuff but sometimes it's the devil of a job. In the Porsche I have had problems with that low Volvo wagon with very wide tyres and been eaten alive by Yamahas. In the Bentley I was, the other day, thwarted by the rev limiter while overtaking a Lexus coupé. My (reluctant) conclusion is: lie back and enjoy the primary advantage of high speed – greatly reduced journey times. The secondary appeal – that special groin-tightening thrill of getting to the edge of the envelope – is, in a modern car, too risky.

You can get the thrill much lower down the scale in a classic.

In Vintage iron the best I recall was an 8 litre Bentley with a narrow fabric body. When I owned it this had run only a tiny mileage, so that all the obscure wearing surfaces that 'restorers' usually forget about were still unworn. You could steer round obstacles calmly at 110 mph. The most unnervingly wandery was a Speed-Model Invicta; this could be half cured by spoiling its appearance with 6.50 × 15 in wheels. Malcolm Campbell's 38/250 Mercedes, 'GP 10', felt dreadful at over 80 mph. The best of post-Vintage metal was the ex-Bira 3½ litre Bentley – the sole car in which I ever crossed the finish line of a race circuit in first place. Incomparably most alarming – the only car in which I had to throw in the towel to a slower one, worn down by sheer terror on the 1989 Scottish Rally – was a 3½ litre SS100.

All this time, of course, the design of road cars was steadily improving. Both the Cadillac 62 and the Buick Roadmaster were very fast, quiet *and* held the road well – unless an unpredictable incident occurred, in which case it would be a case of 'head for the hedgerows'. Then came the D-series Citroëns, and some time later the car that sounded the death-knell of the 'sports' two-seater: the Audi Quattro.

Our hobby is supported by enthusiasts of two kinds: those who like to arrange cars in rows and polish them; and those who like simultaneously to fantasize and frighten themselves. Which sort of custodian do you think a classic car itself prefers?

Cloisters

Monday, 19 January 1981

I found Ian Gow* in the Smoking Room and he took me to the Savoy. Really, his driving in his little blue Mini is now completely berserk. He delights in it, and it makes one's hair stand on end – particularly as he is not a specially skilful driver. At one point as we screamed along the Embankment (it was pouring with rain) I envisaged a terrible accident with the tiny Mini somersaulting across the dual carriageway, an incandescent fireball. He told me that he sometimes drove the Prime Minister in the car with a detective sitting in the back.

★ Ian Gow, Margaret Thatcher's PPS at the time. He resigned from Mrs Thatcher's government in protest at the Anglo-Irish agreement in 1985 and was killed by a car bomb in 1990.

Small cars are all well and good but girls don't like them. Still, a Citroën 2CV ranks as an all-time great

Alan's Citroën 2CV is parked in its own little shed at Saltwood Castle. It's a classic CV – being a 1963 model it has the mad corrugated bonnet and very simple interior, correct early pattern Michelin X tyres and radiator muff, all of which are much appreciated by 2CV purists. The car has clearly not run for a long time but was much enjoyed when on the road. Alan drove it hard and fast, including on long trips from Saltwood Castle all the way to Zermatt in the Swiss Alps! The Citroën represents the underdog and is a real laugh to drive flat out as well as being a perfect tool for humiliating ignorant Ferrari drivers in the snow . . .

This piece brought more outrageous letters than any other because of Alan's reference to Italian car electrical systems which 'appear to have been assembled by handicapped children in a Unicef hostel'. He was sorry this caused such a reaction as he didn't really intend to be nasty. More a case of being carelessly insensitive.

There is something curiously appealing about very small cars. Unless, of course, they are so small that you look slightly absurd driving them. This is almost true of early Austin Chummys (perhaps for that reason they look less ridiculous with the hood up), and is certainly the case when a normal-sized male sits in an MG J2. All of which is very unfair as both of them are pleasing little pieces of machinery, the Chummy in particular being, at its own scale, almost as tough as a Silver Ghost.

Yet the Fiat 'Topolino', whether the early water-cooled four-cylinder version or the air-cooled twin, never looks ridiculous. Gem-like, cheeky, yes; but always interesting. I believe this is because, subconsciously, there is something about the Fiat's appearance that makes you know it is going to handle – not impeccably, but in a manner that will make it fun to drive. Some Italian designers just know how to convey this feeling – *by line* – and it is always valid.

Don't get me wrong. I am not an uncritical fan of all that is Italian. Most of their cars (and that includes most Ferraris) are rubbish. They won't start on a wet day and 'skid' on shiny surfaces. Their electrical systems appear to have been assembled by handicapped children in a Unicef hostel. However, when the Italians really get it right – Lancias Aprilia and Aurelia GT, the Ferraris 166, 340, 410 (racing versions) and the roadgoing 275GTB4 – they are, in their particular ways, the most incredible machines ever built. And somehow, although I find practically every other Fiat loathsome, the 'baby' ones are divine.

It is a paradox that small cars are much easier to make handle properly than heavy ones. And although brute power will get past you on the straight, or on the motorway, you can have so much more fun on the twisty bits. The brakes last longer, too, the lighter you are.

Consider the Cisitalia single-seater when first it appeared on the scene in the 1940s. Or the OSCA 1300 cc sports racers that so often snicked in front of heavier metal – and showed stamina too (one of them won the Sebring twelve hours).

Much the most formidable sports racing car of the mid-1950s was the 2.3 Gordini, in which Jean Behra would regularly cut up the opposition – Jaguar C-types, Aston DB3s and Ferrari 340s. I remember looking at it in the paddock and thinking how *tiny* it was (Behra himself was built like a jockey). What happened to that car? I think Amédée Gordini only built one before he went bust; after being campaigned for two seasons it finally broke – was it in the Carrera Panamericana?

But to revert to road cars, here are the advantages of designer downsizing:

(1) Fuel bills shrink out of sight;

(2) There is always room in the centre lane (especially on two-lane roads);

(3) Parks anywhere;

(4) Drives owners of more expensive cars mad.

The disadvantages?

(1) Female passengers are unkeen.

(2) You get a terrific view of the accident.

(3) Too exhausting for both man and machinery on long journeys. We are talking of course, about nippy midgets.

For serious *de-escalation* – a different and more restful concept – there is only one solution: the 2CV, preferably with left-hand drive and corrugated bonnet. The fuel level never, it seems, alters. The huge, narrow, Michelin Xs last for 50,000 miles. The very simplicity of the heater guarantees that it always works. So you can roll back the giant sunshine roof and waft along, one elbow on the door, with that very soft suspension giving the sensation, almost, of a big US convertible of the 1950s.

Until you come to a corner, that is. Then, if you wish, you may put to the test the maxim that decrees that there is no curve in a country road anywhere in Europe for which you have to lift off in a Citroën 2CV.

I still have my own, bought new and delivered in Lyons in 1963. St Tropez-blue, it now looks as crumpled as last week's packet of Gitanes. Some of the rubber hammock straps have got brittle and snapped, so that the seats have to be padded with discarded garden cushions. Many times it has done the journey from Saltwood to Zermatt and back.

Its high point was overtaking a Ferrari 250 in the winter of 1967. The 2CV had no problem crossing the spine of slush and ice in the centre of the road, while the banker and his girlfriend (I assume that's what he was; the car had Zurich plates) were suffering from the opposite of down-force, as the snow lifted their car's underside while the back wheels span angrily.

The exact location was – I am very mindful of last month's letter quite rightly pointing out that the Witney bypass wasn't finished until 1977; my exploit in the XK was on the then incomplete stretch of the A429 between Wolvercote and Eynsham – on the hill which climbs out of Vallorbe. Anyone got a really low-mileage 1960s 2CV to sell?

Alan Clark is dismayed that the Bentley 'Scalded Cat' never made it into production

Alan once again writes about his favourite Q-cars and is impressed by a Daimler Majestic Major hearse hurrying to the crematorium.

He attacks British manufacturers for not having the courage to produce what the consumer really wants. He thought the Rolls-Royce B80, straight-eight-litre engine would have turned the already good Bentley R-type Continental into a world great. And he's probably right; it is the most tasteful hot rod in which to vanquish all opposition.

Perhaps I have had more fun with Q-cars than with any other kind of vehicle. Particularly with the 1600 cc Porsche-engined, small-window Beetle I described in the September issue; but also, as a student and long thereafter (until – fool, Clark, fool – I sold it to pay for a skiing holiday), with a really battered LHD 1941 Ford Coupé whose engine had been stroked, induction ports polished, and fitted with a 3/4 race cam.

The Michelin X tyre had just arrived on the scene and in heavy duty 6.50 × 16 in form would endow miraculous road-holding once you had taken up the roll (by snicking the Catseyes with your door handles). S1 Bentley saloons, in two-tone colours, were my favourite prey. It's a class war thing, really, isn't it? The prize is the indignant demeanour of the silk-shirted MD, as he has to give best to a rusty something that looks as if it cost less than a full tank for his own car.

Daimler-Benz always realized this. A marketing rule was that no owner of a car in its saloon range should suffer the indignity of being overtaken by a model in the same range costing less.

One day, though, the boot was on the other foot. On the old

Staines bypass we noticed, some distance in front, a vehicle overtaking traffic which obstinately refused to get any closer even though we (in a Citroën Safari) were travelling at either side of 100 mph. What the hell was it? Curious, angular configuration, very accelerative – much better than us in third gear.

Finally, when it was baulked, the strange silhouette of the interior turned out to be a coffin (or chocolate-box, in the vernacular) complete with brass rail surround. It was a long-wheelbase Majestic Major, hurrying to the crematorium.

I never forgot this experience and for several years kept an eye out in breakers' yards for write-offs. I toyed with the idea of putting the engine into a Barker three-seater drophead – which would certainly have elevated that distinguished-looking but ponderous tourer into the *Grand* category. But there were problems at the flywheel end, and to what gearbox you adapt it. Also I wonder if, even then, you could easily get hold of a spare head or even rods and pistons.

That Daimler V8, 4½ litre, with hemispherical combustion chambers and an extraordinarily even power curve, was one of the four finest engines – no, I'd say one of *only* four good engines – made by the British motor industry after the war. And three of them are in the 'why-on-earth-didn't-they?' category.

The great Jaguar twin-cam six, that went on winning races for thirty years, is obviously foremost. But none of the attempts to improve it really worked. So why on earth didn't they put the Daimler V8 into the E-type? This would have reduced weight on the front end, improved the handling and made it still faster – a kind of aesthete's Corvette. Or perhaps that was why Jaguar bought up Daimler – to prevent this happening, like Rolls-Royce stifling the Bentley/Napier at birth.

And what about the beautiful little Coventry Climax four? So light that in static form as a fire pump two men could carry it around, and immensely strong. It and its variants must have powered more race winners than any other engine except the Cosworth V8. But in its original form it was cheap and simple. Could not Morgan at least, have put it in the 4/4?

Rootes had a go, downsizing it for the Imp. But that car was so badly assembled, and its ancillaries so awful, that it never had a chance. All that exercise illustrated was the perennial truth that, if you want to detune an engine, do it by attention to the cam contours, the timing and size of the inlet valve, not by reducing swept volume.

And then the Rolls B80. Only once put in a car – the famous 'Scalded Cat', whose performance so alarmed the board of Rolls-Royce and certain motoring journalists (who should have been ashamed of themselves), including specially respected boobies on the editorial staff of the *Autocar* – that the car was scrapped. Later, a few were put into the Phantom IV, a limousine confined to heads of state, and with a kerb weight of three tons. The only outlets for that wonderful power unit were the Saracen and Saladin military six-wheelers, where they proved more reliable and durable than any competitor.

Imagine that engine, though, in the R-type Continental! From being a leading contender for greatest post-war classic the Bentley would have been out-and-out, untouchable, victor. Why is it that manufacturers, especially here in Britain, so often lose their nerve? They don't just think they know what is best; they decide what is best *for* you. To which the consumer's answer ought to be, 'We'll decide that, thanks very much.' If we, the consumers, were allowed to, there'd be a lot more classics around today.

Cloisters, Westminster

Thursday, 16 July 1981

It always takes longer to get to the American Ambassador's residence in Regent's Park than one anticipates. I was using the old green Bentley as my faithful 2CV is presently immobilized with a puncture. The custodian at the gate said, 'The name must be Clark,' from which we inferred (rightly) that we were the last to arrive.

Driving probably the fastest Bentley R-type Continental in the world?

Q-cars, hot rods and Bentley Specials are all fabulously appealing to drivers who really like to press on. This is a similar feature to one that I wrote for the Daily Telegraph motoring section in May 1999. Alan Clark drove a very fast and subtly improved Bentley R-type Continental alongside his very original example. How did he find the comparison?

Political correctness is not an entirely new phenomenon [writes Robert Coucher]. During the 1950s Britain was still cowed by shortage and rationing after the ravages of World War Two. Times were bleak, especially for the relatively few 'motorists'. Motor cars were predominantly nasty, underpowered contraptions and petrol was scarce and pathetically low grade. Conspicuous consumption was frowned upon as most Britons were 'making do' as best they could.

But Rolls-Royce knew there were enough aristocrats, potentates and playboys who had survived the great conflict with their ample funds intact. It set about building a single-minded, immensely fast grand tourer which would enable this select group to motor to Monte Carlo in time for a brandy and soda before an expensive evening's entertainment in the casino.

So, in 1951 the Bentley R-type Continental was unveiled. Rolls-Royce had taken over Bentley Cars in 1931 to produce more sporting variants alongside its stately saloons and to stop any other manufacturer taking control of this auspicious marque. Bentley's had evolved from making fast lorries (as Ettorio Bugatti referred to them when they humbled his dainty Bugatti racers in the 1920s) under W.O. Bentley's control, to Silent Sports

Cars – the 'Derby' Bentleys – later produced under Rolls-Royce's ownership. But more was needed. The opening up of Europe, with its fast-flowing roads, required an all-conquering machine to re-establish the pre-eminence of the Bentley marque.

The Continental is based on the Bentley R-type saloon chassis but is enveloped entirely in aluminium in a bid to keep the weight down. With this lightweight H.J. Mulliner fastback body-work, the overall weight is 3800 lb, about the same as the new Jaguar S-type, and it's aerodynamically clean with a better drag co-efficient than an E-type Jaguar. The early cars had 4½ litre straight-six engines, later enlarged to 4.9 litres, producing 172 bhp with prodigious torque. The Continental was clocked at 119.75 mph when launched, aided by its long, close-ratio gearing. This made it the fastest four-seater in the world, capable of running with the Jaguar XK120 and other outright sports cars.

Only the most discerning, the wealthiest and the most extravagant could afford to spend £4890 plus a purchase tax of £2038 on a car in the 1950s, a sum that would have bought a very substantial house in the country. The international *Who's Who* of society and the motoring world revelled in this extraordinary Bentley capable of travelling across Europe at a whispering 100 mph all day. The *Autocar*'s road test of 1952 called it 'a modern magic carpet' and testers were impressed with a fuel consumption of around 19 mpg. The 208 examples of the Bentley R-type Continental were probably the finest motor cars produced in this country . . . ever.

A man who knows a great deal about political correctness, exciting lifestyles and socio-political history is the Rt. Hon. Alan Clark, MP. A keen motoring enthusiast, he has owned a Bentley Continental for years. His example is very original and it is known that Alan Clark is not the polishing type – he prefers his antiquities well worn and largely unrestored, just like his residence, Saltwood Castle.

On the other hand, Christian Hueber, registrar of the Bentley Continental Register, is a motoring aficionado who likes his cars immaculately presented. Not content with owning an example of Bentley's best, Hueber has carefully personalized his 1953

Continental. His Connaught-green Bentley is perfection, only more so. The chassis is largely standard, just carefully adjusted for a more sporting response, although a thicker front anti-roll bar has been added as well as one fitted to the back. The engine is balanced and lightened with improved gas flow, a higher compression ratio, three SU carburettors in place of the standard two and a more efficient extractor exhaust. Most of these modifications are out of sight and were, in most cases, tried by the Crewe experimental department. The only way you can tell that Hueber's car is different from standard is by the twin tailpipes and Dunlop racing tyres, as used on the prototype's record-breaking run.

The enticement to Alan Clark was a photograph of Hueber's Bentley, charging along an autobahn with the speedometer reading 135 mph and the rev counter in the red paint at 4000 rpm. It worked. An invitation was extended to visit Saltwood Castle for a test drive, to compare the Hueber car with the Clark Continental. The drive down to Saltwood Castle proved a revelation. The big Bentley, with 203 bhp and a massive 301 ft/lb of torque, is magnificently fast. Only the latest Bentley Turbos are a match. Although long, the car is wieldy in London traffic – it's narrow and you are at eye level with Range Rover drivers. The steering is precise, the clutch surprisingly light and the brakes reassuringly powerful. The right-hand manual gearshift is slick and delicious in operation. With a top speed of over 140 mph, Hueber's Continental will erupt from standstill to 60 mph in a shade under ten seconds. All this is possible from the quiet comfort of Connolly leather seats, Wilton carpeting underfoot and a swathe of carefully hewn walnut, housing the big Smiths instruments. You might expect this level of performance from one of today's plastic missiles but not from a sybaritic four-seater of the 1950s.

Alan Clark is known for his appreciation of originality and patina – his moss-green 1953 Bentley Continental is clearly well loved but appears used and unpampered. In stark contrast to the gleaming Hueber car, it wears its patina with pride, like the imposing and time-ravaged castle. Clark is taken with Christian Hueber's fastidious car but points out that the missing rear-wheel spats add a great deal to a Continental's lines, and he does not hold much truck with them having been removed to aid rear-brake cooling.

Comparisons are drawn and detailed discussions ensue, leading to Clark taking the wheel of Hueber's car. 'I have a demanding route around the castle which I know intimately. It shows up any shortcomings a car might have and gives me immediate insight into its performance and handling,' says Clark as he drives through the castle gate.

Alan Clark is at one with the Continental. His control is obvious, like an expert horseman on a new mount. Gearshifts are matched perfectly to the revs and the Bentley is hustled and extended from the start. He is a very good driver.

'There is significant improvement in this car's handling and stability which makes it much safer at speed than the standard offering,' says Clark. 'It's a result of advancements in engineering knowledge and materials, especially with the very much better racing tyres. Over these roads it feels superb. There is no question this is a dominant machine which will mix with anything on the roads today bar the most extreme sports cars. You have to think of it in competition terms – I can't think of much that will get past it.

'The engine is more powerful than the original but the result is some loss in the silken smoothness Continentals are renowned for. Probably due to the 8:1 compression ratio being significantly higher than the original. You do get the distinct feeling that there is more going on under the bonnet. I am amazed that it has a better fuel consumption figure than the original but this is, again, a function of the higher compression ratio and greater efficiency of the engine.

'This Bentley is extremely fast with a remarkable increase in power – if you put this engine into my car it would be all over the place; it certainly shows great advances over the last forty-five years. I have thought of making my green car faster but Hueber's is a lesson you can't do that unless you improve every-thing else as well – the brakes, tyres and the chassis. I am changing gear about 1500 rpm short of the rev limit, not having seen the torque and power curves, but I'm conditioned to driving my car on its torque, never needing to rev it through to the maximum,' he notes as he confidently flows the Continental through a fast right-hand bend.

'The Continental is one of a few really great, great cars. It ranks with the Rolls-Royce Silver Ghost, the light-bodied Derby Bentley and the Bentley Mark VI, if you can ever find a good one that has not rusted out. I am safe in the notion that my Continental will always start and it never goes wrong. It is the nicest pure Bentley ever made.

'I am delighted that Hueber has done this extensive development to such a fine machine but I prefer my Continental as original because it represents a different period of motoring, with its integral charms intact. I would not desire my car in this state of tune as some of the appealing gentleness is lost. But, saying that, these Bentleys could be ordered from the works in the way preferred by the driver and I'm sure many were specified similarly. I drive my Continental for therapy and still have no trouble with salesmen in Vauxhalls on the motorway. When I feel the need for a sports car my C-type Jaguar or little Porsche 911 provide ample performance.'

Modern Bentleys aren't as bulletproof as you'd think

Alan's beloved Bentley Continental 'S' created mixed feelings with its small annoyances. This piece initiated a number of telephone calls and letters from Rolls-Royce, concerned at the criticism levelled at the Continental. But Alan really loved it.

Of course his Bentley was slightly special in true Q-car style. His was one of the factory specials, fitted with the more powerful S engine, and he'd added his own finishes to make the big and beautiful car look as unobtrusive as possible.

I love my Bentley Continentals. (The 'S' was a limited edition built alongside the Continental 'R', with certain Bentley Azure features such as bigger wheels and the Zytec engine-management system.) But my love is tinged with melancholy, with nostalgia and – sometimes – with an irritation that even turns to hate. True love, in fact.

First, the good things. This modern car is very handsome. The four-door Turbos are giant container-ships, boxy and dated, but the proportions of the Continental are so good it could be any size unless you have something to scale it against. In fact, I deliberately understate the appearance of my own car, having had the shiny wheels stoved matt black, among other minor mods. Unlike (I assume) most owners I don't want other road users to think, 'Look at that rich git in his Bentley' – not until it's too late, anyway.

So at night, parked under a street lamp, it looks vaguely menacing but unflashy – rather like one of Junior Johnson's racing Pontiacs in the 1970s – and this also gives good protection against it getting keyed by a roaming Class War activist.

I love the performance. Under full acceleration the tyres will yelp at every gear change, even from third to top, in spite (unlike the 'R') of it having a viscous axle. The handling is excellent, both predictable and responsive. I also love the heating and ventilation and the seat bum-warmers, and the overpowering sense of insulation from other road users and their problems.

But . . . The brakes are dreadful. You can use them once from 120 mph. After that, accident avoidance is down to eyesight and steering. Like the early XKs. There is no on-board computer. Why on earth not? The only reason I can think of is that even the most overweight Lloyd's broker might wince a bit when he sees his 'actual' fuel consumption is running at 7.68 mpg. Nevertheless, this is a tiresome omission.

The rear window gets very dirty, but there is no way of washing or wiping it while the car is in motion. The headlights are pathetic except on full beam – in which mode every TIR lorry from Westminster Bridge to Dover docks will give you the full treatment. The fuel tank is too small, so turbo-diesels will give better long-range journey times because they can run non-stop.

Some of these are major, some minor, design faults. But in 1997 none should be present in a car costing £50,000 – never mind four times that sum.

And now some tales from my personal experience.

On the dash there are two 'Red Label' logos, one on the speedo, one on the centre console. When the instruments are lit one logo glows, the other is invisible. When I borrowed the prototype in 1992 I pointed this out and suggested that both could be lit for very little effort in production.

'Yes, yes, of course,' was the reply. But when I took delivery of my first car, a Continental 'R' in 1994, the console badge was still dark. I ordered an 'S' in 1995 – 'Perhaps the console badge might now illuminate?'

'Yes, yes. Of course.' Needless to say, it still doesn't. Dutifully I answer the various owner-satisfaction questionnaires that I am sent from Crewe. But this experience reinforces my suspicion that the data therefrom is only put to use when it confirms the prejudices of those who ask the question.

During the summer I was interested in the newly announced

Continental 'T'. I went to Crewe and looked at the production line. Music, shouting, very-far-from-friendly faces. (The previous factory I visited had been the old Porsche 356 shed at Zuffenhausen. Those Germans were like initiates at a monastery: silent, dedicated, intense.) Has Britain always been thus? Recall Rivers Fletcher's disillusion when he started as an apprentice at Cricklewood.

Unattended, a purple 'T' stood with the door open. I looked inside. The dash was half out, hanging on its wiring, and on the (unprotected) cream leather passenger seat lay a hammer.

What the hell was a hammer, least precise of all instruments, the 'Scottish adjusting tool', doing anywhere near that production line? We all know that 'handmade' is now a synonym for 'won't work' – but this was ridiculous.

Last summer on the M3 a discreet avionics ping alerted me to a notice on the dash indicating GEARBOX FAULT. Nothing much happened thereafter except that the engine misfired between gearshifts. If I'd been airborne I would have looked for the nearest diversion runway, but being already on the ground I pressed on to London. Soon, however, the engine actually began to stall between shifts. In St James's Street the engine packed up altogether and with it (of course) steering and brakes. ENGINE MALFUNCTION I was informed, comfortingly.

The agent kept the car for a fortnight but couldn't – or wouldn't – tell me what had happened beyond saying 'computer fault'. 'What computer fault?' I asked. But answer came there none.

Then, just recently, came a low-tech 'malfunction'. The windscreen surround popped out. Very embarrassing. I've never heard of this happening to a twenty-year-old Capri.

This is where the nostalgia bit comes in. When Sir Henry Royce was running the company, even from his villa at Le Cadenet, his personality was so strong that everyone minded their Ps and Qs. Now they are making this wonderful car, the first decent Bentley since its precursor in title of 1952, but who's in charge? Who co-ordinates the detail of design? Does he have the rank to override dissent? Above all, who's responsible for inspection?

Hidden gems once owned by overseas kings, potentates and rulers are waiting to be rescued

'I think that before becoming a serious collector one has to overcome two barriers – one psychological, the other material. You have to think of your motors not as a "second car" or a "third car" as the case may be, but as objects neither convenient nor useful, yet aesthetically pleasing for their own sake, like Old Master drawings or Georgian snuffboxes.'

So said Alan Clark, but he can't disguise his fascination with finding rare and truly original machines that have luxuriated in motor homes, well stored and in near-perfect condition. These 'barn finds' are the stuff of dreams. In many ways Alan enjoys the hunt as much as the aesthetics.

About twenty years ago smart people in the trade (or smartarses, perhaps one should call them) were buying up V12 E-types with delivery mileage only on the clock and putting them in 'barns'. What happened to all these cars I never discovered, nor am I especially bothered. The 3.8 six was far nicer: my general rule of preference decrees that although big engines are fine for pointing and squirting, balance, which is what makes a car flatter the driver, is usually found in smaller packages. In the past I have extolled the 2.3 Gordini and – probably my all-time favourite for 300 miles on a June day in the Alps – the 550A.

Today these E-types certainly won't still be in hibernation, as car traders are what in Stock Exchange parlance are called 'weak holders' – in contrast to dictators, potentates or muddled landed gentry who, as a result of assassination, exile or absent-mindedness, quite often leave incredible treasures in their heated garages. And sure enough I see that on 12 March [1997] Brooks is to sell the Shah of Iran's collection in Geneva: six amazing supercars that between them all have done less than 14,000 miles.

So all-pervading has the cult of the 'barn find' now become that catalogue photographers have actually been known to scatter designer straw over the bonnet and running boards of shabby and otherwise unremarkable 'original' offerings. But it's when you find something genuinely mint, like the Iranian cars, that you realise how phoney and penny-pinching are most '100-point' restorations.

Offhand I can think of several important cars that may (or may not) be in their original locations. When I was a student a male friend and I went to Italy, sharing the fuel costs in my battered Ford V8 convertible. The widow of Count Trossi – who had driven Alfa 158s in the early 1950s – was in love with him, and we spent a few days at her villa, blissfully unaware that the only surviving Mercedes 38/250 SSK with 'Elefant' blower was languishing in her motor house. The car eventually emerged, and was bought by an English earth-moving magnate, but where it is now I don't know.

Still in Italy (rumour only, this one) is the special, unnumbered Ferrari 410 that was built as a reserve car for the 1954 Le Mans team – which is why it was unnumbered, in case it had to be substituted at the last minute . . . After the race it was sold to one of the Marzotto brothers, who in the previous year had won the Mille Miglia. *Locazione*, at present, also *incognita*.

Press on down the Adriatic coast, where you can, for the first time in fifty years, take a ferry to Durazzo in Albania, which was ruled by King Zog and his beautiful queen, Geraldine, until the last war. He had two incredible Mercedes 540Ks, a black four-seater and a white Special Roadster – both still there somewhere, I would guess. Tirana, the Albanian capital, didn't suffer a great deal of damage during the war, and the long period of communist government simply meant that no one was able to drive around very much. I'd be willing to bet that those cars were hidden away safely by loyal palace staff, when Mussolini invaded.

Having snapped these up for black-market dollars, you could gingerly pick your way past the various 'enclaves' in Bosnia and cross the Romanian border. King Carol II, who ruled there from

1930 to 1940, was a great enthusiast. He had a 2½ litre SS100 finished in claret and fitted with chromed outside exhausts (only one other example, registered in England, was so equipped) and double-mounted rear spare wheels. Romania is currently tricky civil-contract-wise, though; some brave prospectors have come to grief there.

You may be relieved to cross the Bosporus and start exploring in Arabia. This territory is a veritable storehouse of exotic low-mileage treasures ... many of them kept, alas, unused for years in garages where ambient temperatures rise daily to 140°F. The paint will have crazed, the veneers have lifted, the leather be as hard and dry as a board but the mechanicals will be unworn.

For more than forty years the sheikhs imported Rolls, Mercedes and Cadillacs, much as the maharajahs did in India in the 1920s. The King of Jordan now keeps most of his cars in England, where they are looked after by the Wood twins. But Nuri el Said, the Iraqi regent disembowelled by the mob in 1958, had some nice machines, including one exceptionally narrow-bodied Phantom IV. There's a good chance of that one, rather too conservative for Saddam's flashy son Uday (now himself crippled by an unsuccessful assassin), still sitting unused in a shed in Baghdad.

Saddest and most tempting of all, though, is the rarest: a Rolls-Royce Phantom III, chassis post-195 DL, despatched in 1940 by the Foreign Office as a mark of favour (bribe) to the Afghan ruler. Somehow, in the course of the Soviet evacuation the car got as far as Kabul airstrip – perhaps they were trying to loot it. The USSR president at that time was Brezhnev – a great car enthusiast but an abominable driver – and there just wasn't room in the last Antonov to leave.

So the Rolls remained stuck on the runway, like the Pucara fuselages at Port Stanley. About six months ago I saw a grainy photo of this car in *The Times*, full of holes from rocket-propelled grenades and Kalashnikovs. 'A Vintage Rolls used for target practice,' read the caption; but I could see that it was a short Thrupp and Maberly tourer with fold-flat screen. Sometimes knowledge can lead to unhappiness.

Jaguar E-types are 'bewitchingly phallic' but let down by British engineering

Alan is a real Jaguar enthusiast. He loved his SS100, his C-type, D-type, XK120 and 140 Coupé but the E-type left him cold. He bought a red E-type roadster for his wife Jane but she didn't care much for it either, especially after she put a ding in the door. The E-type had the flash looks but lacked true dynamic ability, marred by less-than-predictable independent rear suspension and poor build quality.

The first E-type I owned was a 3.8 roadster. Red of course. Buying the car was a monstrous act of self-indulgence because I had two children under the age of four and we had been (just) squeezing all our gear into the Jaguar Mark II that was sur-rendered in part-exchange.

Now the faithful oval-window Beetle had, for the umpteenth time, to come out of retirement for use when we all needed to move around at once. The performance of the 'E' was, in those days, awesome. Too much, really, for narrow tyres and non-positive brakes. I soon found that if I drove the car in relaxed fashion I arrived later than I used to in the Mark II. But if I really used the potential my knuckles were white and I needed up to twenty minutes after arrival before my arms stopped shaking.

My own theory – not based on any engineering expertise – is that the design of the independent rear suspension, conceived for the sedans, induces a mild but unpredictable rear-end steering to an increasing degree as the wheelbase shortens. This phe-nomenon is even more marked in C- and D-type replicas that are fitted with modern IRS instead of their rigid Le Mans axles.

The old XK120, kept even further back in the barn than the Beetle, ran dead straight at its maximum speed (had not, indeed, 'Soapy' Sutton done 172 mph at Jabbeke?). But the E felt dreadfully light at the front, and wobbly at the back, at over 115 or so. This may have been due to superior aerodynamics causing the beautiful nacelle to lift but the effect was the same – whatever had been pressing you (usually a 356) would loom in the driving mirror as soon as you had to start putting on the steering lock.

This may just be a personal phobia, I suppose. But with the exception of the Mercedes sedans (emphatically not the sports car classics, 190 and 300SL), I seldom feel entirely at ease at high speeds in a car with IRS. Indeed, it acts as a kind of speed governor. Range Rovers and Discoverys can rapidly become uncontrollable at over 85 mph if you have to take avoiding or even corrective action – as is testified by the number of unexplained accidents that these vehicles, usually driven by harassed mums, suffer in daylight on dry days on busy motorways.

Some years after I had got rid of the 'E' a friend lent me one of the genuine Lightweights and I disliked it even more than the production version (I believe that, later on, Peter Lindner, a very good Jaguar driver, was to meet his death in that car). And last year I did a comparison test of the 'C', 'D' and lightweight 'E' for the *Daily Telegraph* and found that modern tyre design and rubber compound, plus still harder suspension settings, had done no more than postpone the onset of high-speed anxiety.

I did part-exchange that early E-type for its successor, with the 4.2 engine and all-synchro box. It wouldn't rev so freely but was (even) easier to drive in lazy style, particularly for girls. Yet none of the detail faults had been corrected; the bootlid still flew open every time you went over a French level-crossing, causing small but important bits of luggage to go missing. I took it as far south as the island of Ischia and naturally there wasn't a car in Italy that could get near it. On the return journey over the Simplon I never needed to drop below third gear. Yet on bad surfaces, pavé or potholes the suspension felt weak and the one-piece bonnet shifted and shuddered. This car, I felt, could never do a hard Liège–Rome–Liège – never mind the Carrera Pan-americana.

And so, when I parted with it I felt no pang of disloyalty. I reverted to Porsche 356s whose lovely clunky doors, unburstable engines and ability to run on air after the fuel light came on has caused me to love every single one.

There is a sad truth attaching to the E-type, the most bewitchingly phallic and overpowered sports car of the 1960s: if it had been made by Germans it could have been the greatest classic of all time. As it was, the British artistic genius that devised that line, the designer skills that squeezed a more powerful version of that wonderful twin-cam engine into a chassis 200 lb lighter than its predecessor, were diminished.

Of course, Germans could never conceive anything so beautiful – compare the ME109 with the Spitfire – but if assembled in Dortmund, the E-type would never have fallen to pieces.

Some really good classic cars have vanished from the scene without trace

Here Alan writes thoughtfully about a wide selection of very good machines that he's had the good fortune to drive. He has clearly done a good deal of motoring with them and shows he's far from being a car snob – he understands and appreciates the merits of very different cars ranging from an exotic Delahaye 135 to a rather more mundane Austin Atlantic. Some of the machines that he rates highly are now eschewed by today's classic collectors.

For some years after the war petrol was rationed in Britain, so one of the charms of getting away to the Continent (apart from a strong pound, which would then exchange for 12 Swiss francs) was that as a tourist one could draw fuel for almost unlimited motoring.

At the time I was a teenager and really could barely drive at all. Self-taught, I believed there to be only two positions for a clutch, 'in' or 'out', which made traffic exciting. Many of the cars I used would today be heavy items – some even 'refer department' – in an auction catalogue. Others have since vanished from the classic scene almost without trace.

The very first time I drove across France was in a Delahaye 135, a two-door closed coupé by (I think) Pennock. It had been bought for a song by an army friend and still had Dutch registration. Goodness knows how it had spent its time during the Occupation – but it sure hadn't been sitting still. The suspension was shot (difficult to achieve on a Delahaye) and it smoked so badly that you could smell burning oil inside when accelerating. The engine held together, though, and had that special low-compression smoothness that comes with broken piston rings. The standard French challengers in those days were the Onze Légère or, as we call them, 'Maigret' Citroëns. The Delahaye passed them on the straights but they would reappear as soon as the curves started.

My next journey, bizarrely, was in a car that really has disappeared – the Austin Sheerline. There are still quite a few old Princesses around; they were used by funeral firms and very senior cabinet ministers. But the Sheerline, a quite handsome car with P100 headlights and 'razor-edge' styling like a huge Triumph Mayflower, was lighter and more stylish.

My companion's rich mother didn't want him to go abroad except in a *new* car. So we had ended up with this great black beast, which was practically the only car post-war for which there was no waiting list. The Sheerline used the old Austin 4 litre truck engine, an excellent, durable unit. It never gave any trouble at all. But after 600 miles in northern Croatia the suspension felt like the Delahaye after it had got back from the moon. People thought the Austin was a Rolls-Royce, which raised our credit rating – just as well when driving something that gives 14 mpg.

In 1949 I went in a brand-new Ford V8 convertible, the one with a 'spinner' nacelle. Great fun, but in that car I had a bad accident which, although I suffered no injury, must have saved my life many times since with its lesson seared into the memory bank. That lesson? Signals, or their absence, mean nothing. Just look at the road yourself; and *never* overtake if there is an opening, however unpretentious, in the offside kerb or pavement, because once in 200 times the vehicle in front is going to turn across you and try to go into it.

I had borrowed most of the money to buy the Ford and the insurers were a bit thoughtful about meeting the claim in full. So for the summer of 1950 I used an Austin A90 Atlantic convertible. It offered nice handling as long as the dampers held up – it and Elliot Healeys were the only road cars of the era that were easy to set up in a four-wheel drift – and surprising economy, but was hopelessly let down by its brakes. These were Girling 'hydromechanical' – meaning that when the mechanical rear drums were out of adjustment (about every 500 miles), the whole load had to be carried on the hydraulic front ones, which would fade till the next morning after two stops.

In November 1950 I took delivery of a new XK120, the trusty steed I still possess. After the A90's, its brakes seemed adequate. The Jaguar dominated other traffic and went to Le Mans for four consecutive years. I had a press pass from *Road & Track* magazine and used to drive round the circuit when it was closed. I tested the Omega traps at Les Hunaudières in 1952 at 132 mph (on a 3.27 axle). Once I was married, though, the XK went into semi-retirement and I subsisted on more mundane fare.

Nowadays we use our Citroën DS23 Chapron convertible, which I still believe to be the nicest genuine *touring* car ever built. Occasionally, if we have an enormous load, we take the Discovery TDi, which will go the whole way from Folkestone to Zermatt without refuelling. Once or twice I have gone in the Bentley Continental 'S' but the fuel consumption really hurts, and now the gendarmerie have got the trick of fining you on the basis of average time shown on *péage* slips on the autoroute, much of the point of the performance is lost.

Cloisters

Thursday, 22 January 1981

On the way from the *Telegraph* building to Brooks's, where I was going to meet Euan, and driving somewhat *Frenchly* I just failed to slip inside a red Hillman as he accelerated away from a pedestrian crossing. The occupants immediately put on police caps and flagged me down. They insisted I take a breath test. 'If this bag changes colour one iota I will give you £100,' I said. Of course, looking back I now see that might have been constituted as an overture for a bribe. However, fortunately the celebrated 'crystals' did not alter colour at all. It is somewhat alarming though as one puffs down the plastic tube to see them darkening. This is simply the moisture in one's breath and not the alcohol content, which in my case was nil. All the same, I noted that the division of the colour beyond which a positive reading is indicated and a blood or urine test follows seemed very high up the tube; I got the impression that not much of a drink would get one into trouble.

A little later that evening I went downstairs into Pratt's, which was empty except for, sitting heavily and gloomily in one of those upright circular leather chairs, holding a whisky and soda dark as a piece of mahogany veneer, the Home Secretary [William Whitelaw].

'Ah, Alan', he said, not greeting me with any great warmth.

'I have just been breathalysed,' I said mischievously (breathalysed invariably means '... and produced a positive reading').

But the Home Secretary was very splendid, thundered and spluttered, said it was monstrous, where did it happen, on what grounds did they stop me ... To my delight I realized that he was angry with the police at breathalysing me, not the other way round. I told him that the test had been completely negative and he was almost disappointed. I think that he might well have done something about it if it had been positive. The Drinker's Union.

HOUSE OF COMMONS
LONDON SWIA OAA

13ᵗʰ December 1978

Dear Jack,

On 8ᵗʰ December the Hon
Alan Clark had three cars
parked in the New Palace
Yard Car Park.

Registration Nos:-

CYN 18 C

LKE 418 F

S+A 949

Yours ever,

Victor.

The saga of Alan and the House of Commons car park began when
Victor le Fanu, Sergeant at Arms, wrote to Bernard (Jack) Weatherill,
Opposition Deputy Chief Whip, on 13 December 1978.

HOUSE OF COMMONS
LONDON SW1A OAA

14th December 1978

Dear Alan,

The underground carpark is becomming severely congested and I have just received a note from the Serjeant at Arms drawing my attention to the fact that you have (or had) parked three cars there recently.

The Services Committee laid down that each Member may park one car, and before the matter is raised with the Committee I thought I should draw it to your attention. If you do want to park additional cars may I suggest the underground carpark beneath Church House, Westminster. Members are permitted to park there and I frequently use it myself.

Yours ever

Jack

Hon Alan Clark   MP

HOUSE OF COMMONS
LONDON SWIA OAA

7ᵗ February 1979

Dear Jack,

I am sorry to have to let you know that Alan Clark has a Chevrolet, a Bentley and a Volkswagon in the Underground Car Park to-day. He should have only one car there and I would be most grateful if you could have one more word with him!

Yours ever,
Victor

... Two months later Alan still had three cars parked in the underground car park.

219 4541.   8 February

HOUSE OF COMMONS
LONDON S.W.1.A. O.A.A.

My dear Alan,

I've just received this note from
Victor le Fanu.

I would be grateful if you could ensure
that you bring only one vehicle into
the Underground Car Park. The Services
cttee has a strict rule about this & I
think it would be unhappy for the issue to
appear on our next agenda because that
might cause all kinds of side problems.
The underground car park below Church House
is available to members & it is not widely
used. Can you not shove the chevrolet
& the Bentley in there?!! Yours ever
                                    Jack

. . . There is no record that Alan responded.

83

A press pass can get you into the top motor racing events and even on to the closed circuit for a couple of quick laps

When Alan turned his hand to motoring journalism in the early 1950s, he managed to 'bamboozle' (his word) the American motoring publication, Road & Track, *into appointing him European Correspondent, with his name and address published on the contents page. He held the appointment for about a year. This was a great way of getting his hands on press passes, thus securing entry into the heart of race meetings and the closest trackside vantage points. Here, from the January 1953 issue, is his report titled 'Sports Car of the Year'.*

Now that the European season is drawing to a close it may be of some interest to evaluate *sports car* performances in the major races and attempt to draw some conclusions. I shall try to avoid the method, which is adopted in some quarters, of awarding marks for first, second, and third places in a selected group of races because there are so many variables – differences in length and quality of a circuit, duration of the race, degree of competition, etc. – at each individual event. Instead, I shall attempt to convey some overall impressions.

It has not been easy to pick out any contender this year and say 'that car is unbeatable' as could be said last year of the C-type Jaguar. But there is no doubt that *best performance* has been put up by the 300SL Mercedes. Its record, in fact, bears a curious resemblance to that of the Jaguar in 1951, in that it won at Le Mans after its immediate rivals had blown one another up and mopped up a couple of domestic races in which foreign competition was negligible. (One may compare the Prix de Berne and the Nurburgring with the Silverstone one-hour and the

T.T.) The only race in which Mercedes was defeated was the Mille Miglia – which was the only other event that it tackled this year.

The qualities of the 300SL are not of the spectacular kind. The engine design is straightforward, with single overhead cam-operated valves sucking in just three litres of gas per cycle; nor is there anything radical about the chassis, with its swing axle IRS, whose antecedents are apparent in previous Mercedes designs. In my opinion, the qualities of the Mercedes are secondary rather than primary, that is to say they lie in meticulous preparation and assembly of every moving part, immense thoroughness in testing and painstaking attention to the smallest detail. The layman might think that these are essential to any team of racing cars but it is only Mercedes who seem really to understand the meaning of the word 'thorough'. However, these are factors which tell more in a long race like Le Mans and the Mille Miglia, and how well the Mercedes would fare in a short savage tussle with C-type Jaguars and Ferrari 2.9s remains to be seen.

It was particularly unfortunate that the 300SL did not run in what was quite easily the toughest *short* sports car race of 1952 – the Grand Prix de Monaco on 1 June. The course is extremely dicey and includes a vicious downhill section containing three hairpin bends, a 100 mph curve *through a tunnel*, and a back leg between the houses of Monte Carlo and over very indifferent surfaces. On the starting grid were displayed the cream of European sports machinery – no fewer than fourteen Ferraris at the peak of their tune (being only a few-score miles from their home garages across the frontier), Cad-Allards, C-type Jaguars, DB3 Astons, OSCAS, Lago-Talbots, Frazer Nashes, and – the Gordini. This fantastic little car is, in my opinion, the most outstanding sports car of 1952 and its performance in the Monte Carlo race was characteristic. After getting the go-ahead signal from its pits, it caught up Moss, who was leading in the XK-C at the rate of seven seconds per lap (in spite of Stirling's receiving speed-up signals from his own pit). However, no sooner had it taken the lead than it was eliminated in the multiple crash which also involved Moss's Jaguar, Parnell's Aston, and Hume's Cad-

Allard and robbed the race of much of its interest, making it a Ferrari procession.

To uphold the Gordini on a results basis is not easy as it has not yet won a single race, but it is also true to say that it has never entered a race in which it has not taken the lead before retiring. The only exception to this is the Nurburgring event where it seized its driveshaft when lying second. Its dazzling performance at Le Mans was the highlight of the race. If one were to attribute this success to any single factor it would be – low weight, repeat, *low weight*. The old idea that a car has to be heavy to hold the road well is right out of date. Everybody realizes this now but few apply the principle so drastically as Gordini.

I shall never forget standing at Arnage on the first lap of the Le Mans race this year: Walters in the Cunningham coupé was the first to arrive, with Moss hanging on his bumper ... There was a short gap and then a thick bunch of tough boys all jostling fiercely; right in among them was this tiny little blue car. I thought at first it was a 750 cc Dyna Panhard and couldn't believe my eyes when I saw it out-accelerate Spears' Cunningham! The answer is that it must be one of the very few two-seaters in the world that gives 300 bhp per ton. The kerb weight of the car is little more than 11 cwt and the 2.3 litre twin overhead cam engine gives all of the 160 hp with 7500 revs available to those who wish to hang onto their indirect gears. And don't forget that being only half as wide as a Cunningham it has twice as much road to drift in. It takes my money as the most attractive sports car of the year and the most advanced design. In 1953, when there are more about and when the lessons learnt on this year's prototype have been applied, it should cause a lot of trouble to Mercedes and Jaguar teams.

No one can maintain that Jaguar have had a good year. Their performance at Le Mans was most disappointing – heartrending indeed when one reflects that a team of production XK-Cs might easily have won the race as last year's record was beaten by only sixty-eight miles and Walker and Whitehead had been limiting themselves to 4900 rpm from 2 a.m. when the opposition faded. However, that is much too big an *if* to enter in our calculations. The fact remains that the only Continental event which Jaguar have won this year was the Prix de Rheims where Moss made the Talbots look pretty silly but was himself trailing the Gordini (at all too respectful a distance) until it crashed. Does this mean the XK–C is getting obsolete? I don't think so, quite. The disc brakes are clearly the best anchors available in racing today. They were not fitted to the Le Mans cars as under certain conditions the hydraulic fluid boiled and generally got out of hand but this problem seems to have been overcome now. Nonetheless, the C-type is not cock o' the roost to the same extent as last year and I think it highly probable that at least one car will carry the 4½ litre engine at Le Mans in 1953 or else the 3½ engine will be housed in a very much lighter chassis.

To form a fair opinion of Ferrari performance is not easy as there is no factory team in sports racing – though the entry of such an *équipe* has long been rumoured to be imminent – and opinion can only be based on the performance of private owners' cars under different conditions. Bracco won the Mille Miglia in a car reputedly experimental and of 3 litre capacity, which is subsequently believed to have been Ascari's mount at Le Mans in which he held the lead intermittently from the fourth until the fifteenth lap and broke the lap record before he retired with clutch trouble. A bevy of 2.7 litre Ferraris mopped up the Monaco race after the multiple crash mentioned above; were badly beaten (even by DB3 Aston Martins) at Boreham, but defeated other reputedly more reliable makes in the BARC nine-hours. The Carini 4.1 litre was made to look very foolish by the Mercedes at the Nurburgring, but Daetwyler's 4.1 had lapped faster than all the Mercs at the Bremgarten although he broke his transmission at the starting line on race day. To generalize one might say that the nearer they are to Modena and home the better they go. The quality of individual drivers varies very greatly and the Ferrari still seems to have a few weak points in the chassis unless it is driven very gently or very skilfully. There is no doubt, however, that should Signor Ferrari give the word and the factory apply themselves to disciplining and maintaining a sports car team it will prove extremely hard to beat. They may well be forced to do this next year if the Mercedes invasion spreads — particularly if privately owned Mercedes start trouncing private Ferraris as may well happen next summer . . . for 300SLs are already being delivered to customers in Switzerland.

No revision of the season's events would be complete without mention of the Alpine Rally. 'Sports cars' in the major events today are, to all intents and purposes, two-seater racing cars utterly devoid of elementary comforts necessary for a touring car (the one exception being the Mercedes, even their Le Mans cars being beautifully upholstered and finished). But the 'Alpine' really is contested by cars that the public can buy and you can be sure that those cars that win cups are the fastest *and* the most rugged in their class; some indication of the severity of the trial as a chassis breaker is the number of retirements with such hefty fractures as a broken stub axle or a collapsed wheel. It should also be noted that the Sunbeam Talbot team which did so well was a 'works' entry, the cars being specially built and prepared at the factory while all the other British entrants were private owners. Outstanding performances which may escape notice by their omission from the list of finishers were Mackenzie's Ford Zephyr (British light ohv 6) which made fastest 3-litre time on the Stelvio against the Sunbeams, and a DB2 Aston Martin and Imhof's Cad-Allard which retired on the last day with mechanical failure. However, with Gatsonides making best time of the day in all but one of the daily climbs and Appleyard making best time in the final breaking and acceleration test, one cannot but cite the trusty XK120 as being still the finest day-to-day touring sports car. The stamina of that car is really extraordinary.

As for the out-and-outers, it is as I have explained rather difficult to form a clear opinion because they have so rarely been all together in joint competition this year. The Gordini is undoubtedly the fastest. The Mercedes the best combination of speed and reliability, the others − ? Not outclassed, yet. But a little more discipline and organization from Ferraris, from Jaguars a little more luck and attention to detail in about equal proportions, and 1953 should see some very tough struggles.

Huge engines simply provide absolute and delicious power

As he was such a patriotic Englishman, it is a surprise to find that Alan liked American cars so much. German and French machines are understandably appreciated for their engineering and excellent suspension but Alan really preferred his Buick, Pontiac and Oldsmobile for their big, smooth and relaxed engines, their friendly demeanour and tough bodies. But mostly for their smooth power delivery.

This appreciation of American iron dates back to when his parents used to run cars from across the Atlantic. Just after the war British cars were generally small and underpowered, and were kept that way by the tax on engine bore size. Those wealthy enough would drive American cars, which were much larger, with powerful engines.

In my early days as an enthusiast I was a fervent advocate of the truism that 'there is no substitute for cubic inches'. This derived partly from my own experience with American cars of the 1930s, which never went wrong and, when we last had a Labour government, could be bought very cheaply by an impecunious student.

Later, as the motorway network spread, these valiant old things, already three parts worn out and being impractically low-geared in top, started to blow up. Even so, one of my all-time favourites, a Buick Phaeton of 1936 or so, with a straight-eight engine of just over 4 litres, still gives a lovely drive. It lives in Scotland now and, with its high ground clearance and docile slow-running, is brilliant on forest tracks. The driving technique is the exact opposite and is contrastingly restful to the full RAC

Special–Stage method. If you never let the engine rise over 800 rpm the wheels won't spin and the cylinder layout means that there will always be one piston at the top of its cycle, so it's practically impossible to stall.

Later on, as my sophistication level advanced, I discovered the concept of *balance*. There is more to driving than that delicious feeling of sensing a car surge forward literally in time with the pedal going to the floorboards.

Also, the addition of cubic inches is subject to the law of diminishing returns. Up-engining the Mark II Jaguar from 2.4 to 3.4 transformed it into one of *the* great sedans of all time. But the enjoyment graph flattens, then may even turn down. Why else is it that, for example, on the road the 7 litre Cobras are really quite nasty, while the original 4.7 litre cars are great fun? All engines have their own idiosyncrasies – vibrations, flat spots and 'periods' – and on very big engines these are amplified.

So the solution is to keep the revs as low as possible. (By 'keep' I mean design for maximum power and torque points.) Hence the pleasure of light Edwardian chassis adapted to very early aero engines.

This is the reason that the Maybach engine – originally built for the Zeppelins – is so much more pleasant to drive behind than the Merlin, built in the late 1930s. Just recently, Rolls and Bentley specialist Nick Harley has built himself the most beautiful adaptation of a Rolls-Royce Phantom II. The replica Gurney Nutting sedanca coachwork is of the very highest quality. But the whole concept is ruined by a huge boiling, belching Merlin shuddering with impatience at having to wait even for three minutes in the take-off queue at Duxford and eager to get into the sky and chase the Heinkels. Nick would have been better advised to install a 6.7 litre V8 from a Bentley Turbo R write-off (I imagine that with increased City bonuses there must be a few of these around in the scrapyards).

The most successful of the Edwardian monsters is the 1910 Métallurgique. This car really went. And in the days when it was owned by Douglas Fitzpatrick I recall him challenging me to an acceleration test against my (short-chassis) Mercedes-Benz 600. Piece of cake, I thought. Embarrassing. Mustn't rub it in, etc. In fact we started the two cars side by side on the main runway at Keevil airfield. My foot was flat on the floor but the 'Met' stayed in exactly the same position (that is, next to the driver's door handle of the Mercedes) all the way up to 120 mph. The only thing that seemed to alter was the speed of the outside scenery.

Yet the interesting thing is that people who try to *contrive* aero-engined monsters never seem to get it quite right. They assemble the correct basic ingredients – T-head engines, willowy chassis – but perhaps because they can't resist the occasional tiny solecism, the 'concession to practicality/convenience', there is always something about the result that makes it phoney. Either the wheels are too small, the driving position too low – or the brakes are too effective.

Without doubt the finest and most beautifully engineered of them all is the Napier-Railton, specially built by John Cobb to attack the outer-circuit records at Brooklands. Thanks to owner Lukas Huni, I recently reacquainted myself with this vehicle – one of the greatest pieces of automotive machinery in the world. The sheer quality, the nickel steel trunnions, wired lock-nuts and double cantilever springing illustrates the huge gap between something built to average 190 mph for twenty-one hours, a record it still holds, and some 1970s bodge-up with a Napier Lion bolted into a Vintage Bentley frame.

Even so, for the total solution, the ultimate Cubic Inch Special, why not consider a tank engine? Unlike aircraft engines, which are designed to run at constant speeds, tanks have to creep, go flat out and withstand *abuse*. The greatest, the T54 – 38 litres and a dry weight of one ton – was also built in the largest numbers. It gave half the power of a 1990 Challenger but from twice the swept volume. If it ever goes wrong (unlikely) the handbook is in Cyrillic.

Classic cars can be temperamental but some Ferraris are possessed of more sinister traits

Alan despises modern Ferraris; they are never really driven as everyday cars and tend to be bought by poseurs with a preference for gold chains and slip-on shoes. He asserts that the best road-going Ferrari was the 275GTB/4, a view that is shared by five-times Le Mans winner, Derek Bell, who had one as his daily driver when he was with the Ferrari team in the 1960s. Bell regrets selling it even today, while Alan regrets not buying the Villoresi Ferrari 340MM Coupé, especially as he imagines that the car ended up being over-restored in America and then driven very slowly by a 'collector'. These sorts of thoroughbreds take revenge...

This is Ferrari's anniversary year. Yes, yes, we all know that, and I've had it up to here with hype and posing and gosh–aren't–they–incredible. Can I put the contrary view? I start with a basic question – do you actually know, or know of, anyone who uses a Ferrari every day?

Quite. Do you know of anybody who regularly uses a Ferrari to get around (I mean *journeys*, not mini–trips to the car park of your neighbouring polo ground or upmarket country club), even on weekends?

Perhaps this is an unfair question to pose concerning a classic. But much of the Ferrari hype is founded on the premise that these cars are *instant* classics: only a limited production run, going straight to a premium, three–year waiting list, all that (it always amazes me that whizzo bond–dealers who make millions spotting trends and reading entrails in the financial markets will fall for any old guff from a salesman on the showroom floor).

Actually, you can have more fun on a day-to-day basis with a Datsun 240Z – preferably one with triple DCO30s and wider wheels – or practically any 911.

I think Ferrari only made one really good road car – the 275GTB4 in the 1960s. The marque's mystique depends on some truly epic sports racers, very few in number, and each one built with its own individual (and often far from amiable) character. Leonard Setright has expounded on Modena's archaic and slipshod chassis design in the 1950s.

But those wonderful Lampredi V12s could only have been built, and blessed, by Italians. Each engine was slightly different, and each chassis was endowed with an individual personality – or, as journalist John Bolster used to claim in all seriousness, a soul.

The most vicious car I've encountered – irresistibly so, surpassing even a 1932 4½ litre low-chassis Invicta that tried to kill me on the Steeple Ashton–Melksham road in 1968 – was a Ferrari 340 Coupé built for Villoresi.

Now the 340 was a very dangerous machine. I have personally seen it do for two drivers in races – Pagnibon at Hyères in the 1953 twelve hours, and Tom Cole at Le Mans. But when, forty-five years later, I drove this coupé, I realized that what it demanded was not so much skill (this it assumed as of right) but *respect*. 'Came alive' is an overworked phrase but is the only way to describe what happened at 4000 rpm. For the next 3000 it was leading *me*: potholes, adverse camber, unexpectedly tightening radii ... Don't panic, just lean further forward in the saddle.

Strange, this, because in its appearance the little 340 was quite demure – petite, almost, beside its ugly sisters, those 375 team cars that defeated the Hamilton-Rolt D-type at Le Mans in 1954. They, surely the most brutish, macho racing cars since the SSKL Mercedes, were actually more stable on the road, after redesign with a transaxle and de Dion rear end.

That 340 was one of the few cars I nearly bought and now bitterly regret having missed. I think it must have ended up in America. The reason, of course, was that I didn't want to write the cheque; the excuse, that it had been retrimmed in black leather instead of the correct blue flannel cloth – which, incidentally, can still be found. The minor matter that the cockpit filled – and I mean *filled* – with blue smoke at peak revs I attributed to a blocked crankcase breather and did not consider important, although I did, of course, try it as a reason for reducing the asking price. I expect some restoration shop in the States has by now conned the new owner into rebuilding the motor and the car will never be the same again.

I have often noticed that cars which have been driven to great achievement by heroes of former times do not take kindly to being cosseted in their afterlife. I was once in a rally in which a very famous and historic machine participated. It had been restored authentically, at least as far as the eye could see. But it went very, very slowly – certainly by comparison with its exploits over the same route in the past. After a few days of this humiliation the car took revenge. It broke its owner's arm when he went to crank the engine.

Great Ferraris all had this characteristic, I think. I have a particular soft spot for the 750 Monza, and once spent an afternoon on the Abetone pass with Ferrari works driver, Sighinalfi. The car was brand-new, a mere twelve hours old, immensely lovable, and I treated it gently. He was cruel, unfeeling, needlessly impatient in 'breaking' his steed. Maybe he was trying to show off to an Anglo-Saxon. Ten days later I was in Florence and saw a tiny paragraph on the front page of the *Corriere*: 'Ferrari star dies on the Abetone'. Inside was an illustration – it was the same car.

Buyers beware: there's a difference between the meaning of 'restored' and 'presented'

The subject of restoration is anathema to Alan as it is usually only applied to the external bits of a car while the mechanicals are left to harbour all sorts of defects, which will only come to light if and when the cars are driven good and hard.

Alan really enjoyed the fact that his Rolls-Royce Silver Ghost was the scruffiest car to take part in the 1993 Alpine Commemorative Rally. It was also one of the fastest and did not let him down.

The Alpine Rally was first held in 1912 and Rolls-Royce was humiliated when its cars, 'the best in the world', could not manage to climb the steep Alpine passes. Rolls returned the next year with lighter bodywork and a four-speed gearbox, winning the Team Prize in 1913. The overall winner was Audi.

Alan also writes about replicas in this column. He is being a little disingenuous in referring to his Silver Ghost as an Alpine Ghost. Rolls-Royce produced five Alpine Eagles Team Cars but his is not one of them. It started life as a very ornate and heavily bodied limousine, which he bought as a chassis, then fitting very minimal and light bodywork that made it fast and nimble on the Commemorative Rally. It certainly is all Rolls-Royce Silver Ghost but not in its original form.

I don't know what 'restored' means – shiny, I suppose. However, you should be aware of a new word minted by the auction houses – 'presented'. This word is used by auctioneers, almost always prefixed by the adjectives 'very well' or 'beautifully', to get them off the hook in case buyers complain – after getting their 'restored' purchase back to a garage and jacking up the vehicle to find that the rear axle's rubber bushes have transmogrified into a teaspoonful of black powder.

'Very well/beautifully presented' always puts me on guard. In extreme cases you can still smell the paint thinner from where, until two hours before viewing started, people have been trying to remove overspray from, say, the windscreen surround. And in truth, I'd rather have something 'badly presented', or even 'very badly presented', that goes like a rocket.

The first thing to realize about 'restorations' is that the bits that get the least attention are those that are hardest to get at, or even to see. I have a dealer friend whose idea of restoring a Derby Bentley is to spend up to £10,000 on the coachwork and chrome, to add new discs from DelMar at £2000 a set, plus the addition of four tyres.

The engine? That's the least costly item. Give it a good bath in Gunk, stove-enamel the cam cover, and add a little cadmium-plating here and there, plus a new chrome exhaust tailpipe, and there you are . . . 'Hardly used sir, the previous owner only took her out on fine days.'

The great thing about any engine made by Rolls-Royce is that unless you actually put a hole in the crankcase (quite difficult) they will always keep running – for a bit.

I well recall a fine summer afternoon at Saltwood when we had just induced the engine of a magnificent Phantom II tourer, bought very cheaply, to tick over after thirty years in storage. The great creature stood on the lawn, puffing gently, while doves cooed. Idyllic, really.

Then one of my sons, idly scratching with a screwdriver at the flaking paint on the cylinder head below the header tank inlet, caused a jet of water to spurt out with great force. Water was distributed generously over the entire engine bay from huge fan blades, rotating at 450 rpm. The coil and distributor began to malfunction and the plug leads shorted. Yet thanks to a mouthful of chewing gum and a tiny squirt of aerosol matt black, the car was sold four days later.

Caveat emptor, old boy. About a year later I saw the car in a showroom, looking magnificent, and offered at exactly ten times what I had sold it for. I doubt if the head had been changed and, anyway, would the new owner ever have noticed? Once 'restoration' passes a certain point people seldom drive the cars, except for that tiny distance – which chewing gum on a crack will usually cover – from the trailer to the judging line-up at a concours.

But if you want to get your classic fit for real rallying, or long-distance events like the Mille Miglia, then the bill will be huge – and the finished car will look no different, maybe scruffier, than a Pebble Beach entrant that is about to boil as it moves across the paddock.

The most enjoyable rally I have competed in was the Alpine Commemorative for Silver Ghosts in 1993. We climbed the equivalent of Mount Everest three times, and no entrant's car blew up. Another was the Hamilton rally in 1995 – it was all sports racing cars, private owners and bending rev-counter needles. In both these events the cars were totally genuine, and enjoying their second youth. But a cult is growing of building 'replicas', so that people can enjoy the sensation of dicing with death in the 1950s and 1960s but without the risk of breaking something precious.

A good idea. Why is it, then, that 'replicas' are never wholly satisfying? (With one exception, of course, in which the word is correctly used – namely the Frazer Nash Le Mans Replica, which is exactly contemporaneous with its competing brother.)

For that reason, I suppose – namely that it is practically impossible to 'replicate' an original years after its creation. You may remember, when Ferraris were worth seven figures, a Japanese tycoon giving a 250GTO to his engineers with the instructions to copy it, ten times over, and to get it right, whatever the cost.

They couldn't. Not even the Japanese, the world's best imitators and the finest precision engineers. And the disassembled 250GTO bits are still lying around somewhere.

That is the real problem, I suppose. Replicas ought to be fun, and they are *quite* fun, to drive. But basically they are just imitations.

All you ever wanted to know about the Rolls-Royce Phantom III

Alan is in full anorak mode here, giving chapter and verse on the Phantom III's history, design and maintenance. His knowledge is copious and he rates the Phantom as a truly great car. But unless they are scrupulously well looked after, they can prove unreliable.

Sadly, this piece appears to be incomplete but is worth including for the information it does contain.

Historical origins

While it is true to say that the reputation of the Rolls-Royce company was (and remains) founded on unusually high standards of detail, workmanship and quality of materials, the initial impetus that brought these features to the notice of the public came from the bold, one-model policy which the company launched in 1908 with the Silver Ghost. Over a period when other manufacturers of luxury cars offered a wide range of sizes in engine and chassis (at one time there were no fewer than eight alternatives for the buyer of a Delaunay Belleville), Rolls-Royce made only one chassis – the biggest, at any rate as far as British manufacturers were concerned.

By the later 1920s, however, there was nothing remarkable about six cylinders. Indeed, the Rolls image was under a fiercer pressure from its rivals than at any time until, perhaps, the advent of the 600 Mercedes in the mid-1960s. Many of the qualities that had reached their apotheosis in the superb Alpine Eagle of the late Edwardian era had become mildly devalued under the influence of consumer demand and manufacturing convenience. In only one respect were the New Phantom and Phantom II superior: in their magnificent four-wheel servo braking systems. The overhead valves were never so quiet as on the L-head Ghosts: the engines revved higher; the gearing was lower; the gearbox was integral with the power unit; and the noise of indirects would obtrude when the chauffeur had to change down. Chassis weight crept up as 'strength' was built in, to prevent the elaborate coach-built bodies cracking from frame-whip at high speeds. The decline was barely perceptible, but it could not be denied by the connoisseur.

There had been some improvement with the later Phantom IIs; the bodies were now mounted on a sub-frame, with the concomitant that protective weight no longer had to be built into the chassis frame proper, and the Continental model would exceed 90 mph. But this was not a very conspicuous advance for twenty years of design development – only a 10 mph increase in maximum speed, with the driver cooped low down behind a 10-in windscreen, when the crews of the Alpine Eagles had wafted along sitting 'above the traffic'. At this time, too, the Hispano-Suiza, the 8 litre Bentley and the 38/250 Mercedes all offered a better performance, and several American cars a similar one – yet with markedly greater comfort; the Duesenberg was superior in both respects. It was plain that a radical redesign, of both engine and suspension, was overdue.

Conception and design

The chassis of the new car was the first Rolls to have independent suspension at the front, with a layout similar in both principle and detail to that current on the senior cars in the General Motors line. By contemporary lights it was completely orthodox; and only the detail, finish, massive brake drums and right-hand gear change hinted that this was the most expensive chassis in the world.

The engine, on the other hand, was outstanding – not least in its appearance: a huge sixty-degree V12, whose twin banks, beautifully stove-enamelled, exhausted into flat and narrow manifolds, horizontally ribbed with a kind of sculpted beauty currently available only on the type 57 Bugatti.

Technically, the power unit was a paradox. The company had gained considerable experience of aero-engines and multi-cylinder problems in general during the Great War, and its aero division had kept its reputation alive in the late 1920s and early 1930s with the superb Schneider Trophy power units for Supermarine. Multi-cylinder units had been considered, and rejected, for the Phantom II, and it is hard to believe that the motives that led to their rejection were not at least partly responsible for the manner in which the potentialities of the new engine were, quite literally, choked.

To understand the design environment of the V12, we must first consider the case of the most successful engine made by the company since the Ghost – namely, the 20/25. This unit had proved very sweet and reliable in the small Rolls and had quite altered the character of the 20. In a new chassis, and with a more generous induction system, it was proving outstanding as the 3½ litre Bentley. By, as it were, banking two of these units together, the design department was able to save a lot of development time in such fields as cylinder head design, gas flow, piston and connecting rod dimensions, as well as in many of the other concealed problems of a reciprocating mass. In regard to certain other fundamentals of a multi-cylinder 'V' engine – such as valve operation and cooling lubrication, they had the accumulated experience of the Eagle and Kestrel aero units on which to draw.

Unfortunately, while many of the complexities of the multi-cylinder aero engines were not avoided, the insistence of the sales department on absolute silence and a low, straight torque graph meant that the output potentialities of the engine were ignored. For example, an inaudible tick-over was achieved by a combination of tortuous induction passage and exhaust back-pressure, so brutal that it would have stalled any other engine on the market. While the piston area was some 40 per cent greater than that of its six-cylinder predecessor, the venturi area (by no means over-generous on the Phantom Is or IIs) was increased by a meagre 12 per cent. Such ruthless derating of a large-capacity engine is, of course, a recognized method of achieving long life and constant tune. To match the new engine, the company produced a wonderful gearbox – dead silent on all its ratios, and with syncromesh on second gear (a luxury that had been hitherto denied to owners and their drivers).

The result was a car that felt like, sounded (if that is the word) like and drove like an up-to-date version of the Silver Ghost – which was, of course, exactly what had been intended. In fact, the Phantom III was immeasurably superior to the Ghost in all but one respect. A perfect Phantom III is without doubt the most delightful and satisfying car that the connoisseur can drive, even today. In this car, it seemed, everything was in balance, right through from its performance and the manner of its response to the driver's whim, down to details of the seating position, the secondary controls and the various subdued sounds and moods with which the great car would greet each new day.

Not since the advent of the Ghost had one car stood so clearly above its contemporaries in terms of speed, refinement and appearance. No car could at the same time dominate the highway and command the awestruck respect of the city dweller in the same way as the Phantom III.

But the one field in which it failed to measure up to the standard of the Ghost was critical, and assumed a mounting importance with the passing years: its dependability and ease of maintenance.

Service, modifications and maintenance

The fundamentals of chassis and suspension proved completely reliable, and capable, like all Rolls-Royces, of absorbing considerable punishment and neglect without protest. Early in the car's career, a test rig was driven across the Sahara from the Mediterranean coast to Kano without ill effect (a journey that may be the subject of much wistful pondering by present-day Phantom III owners who suffer from overheating) and the only significant production modification that followed was altering the position of the petrol pumps (on post-AX series cars).

In contrast to the chassis, the engine had certain built-in weaknesses which time and abuse were to bring to light. First, the valves were operated through hydraulic tappets, which tended to stick if dirt became mixed with the oil that actuated them. This could be avoided if two small filters high up in the block were cleaned at the prescribed intervals – but of course they seldom were – and the difficulties were compounded if the sump oil was not changed scrupulously and often. In addition, the effort of turning against twenty-four pushrods proved to be rather too much for the camshaft, which rapidly wore its contours down to a gentle parabola, thus detuning the engine further (by, say, 40,000 miles). Another weak spot in the valve operation was the fibre slipper wheel, which had a fatigue life of between 30,000 and 50,000 miles; when it broke, without warning, the engine stopped and a substantial disassembly job was necessary.

These faults were cured by subsequent modifications on production cars, and owners of earlier models had their engines modified at reduced charge. But the valve operation was never really satisfactory until the introduction of the DL series in 1939, the 'modified' or solid-tappet conversion being neither as silent nor as fast as a hydraulic system in perfect condition.

More serious, though less immediately apparent, was the tendency of the cooling system to develop blockages, due to the number of small passages that collected scale and sediment. The Phantom III had been designed with aluminium cylinder heads, in contrast to the iron head on the 20/25, in order to save weight and to achieve better heat convection. Oxidization of the aluminium, particularly in cases where engines had stood drained for long periods, or where the wrong choice of antifreeze solution had been used, further aggravated the sedimentation problem.

This is where Alan's script ends. He clearly rates the Phantom III highly, but does acknowledge the design is over-complicated, the engineering suffers some inherent faults and the cars do require inordinate amounts of maintenance. – Robert Coucher.

While the Porsche 911 is a superb machine, the 356 is one of the greatest

As with the Jaguar, and the E-type in particular, Alan debunks the myth that the 911 is the best Porsche ever — he prefers the earlier although slower 356, which has more character and personality.

And with 356s Alan's favourite model was the 356 Cabriolet and the 356A Damen. The Damen (German for woman) was the least tuned of the range with a soft engine, but it made up for its lack of outright power and speed by being so sweet and gentle to drive. The soft-top Cabriolet offered the joy of open motoring, but with the substantial hood up it was as weatherproof as any of the coupés. Alan's 356s were always totally reliable and constructed like little jewels.

The 911 has only one perpetual fault — the windscreen wipers. They are so obtrusive, and block the view down that stubby, sloping bonnet. You only realize this when sitting in a 550A, which doesn't have any.

Is this too personal an objection? When I took delivery of mine, from Hahn in Stuttgart, I pointed out this defect, which is a straightforward ergonomic design fault carried onwards from the 356, and the salesman said scornfully: 'If we are still making old-timers to satisfy popular demand you mustn't expect us to try and bring them up to date.' And that was in 1985. Now the only remaining place to get a new old-timer is Malvern, and somehow I think that, splendid though they are, you won't ever find Morgans taking the first three places in the Californian Baja.

In the 1920s and 1930s there were plenty of cars which you could take straight from the showroom and compete in — perhaps this is the best definition of a sports car. Some, like Bentleys and Delahayes, were posh. Others, like HRG and Frazer Nash, were cheap, particularly when second-hand.

The most outstanding was the BMW 328, and it is to this car that the 911 is most easily compared. Brilliant performance, total reliability – and likely to be worsted, on the track or up the hill, only by out-and-out sports-racers.

I never get into my own without some pleasing anticipation, no matter what kind of journey lies ahead.

Let me first list the things it has never done: gone wrong; been overtaken (except by superbikes); returned less than 29 mpg; rattled; let in water (it's a cabriolet); and not arrived early for an appointment.

Even so, it is a melancholy thought that it can never be replaced, as the production line has closed for the August holidays and will not reopen. I suppose I shall just have to go on using mine until it breaks in half. I'm not really interested in a Porsche cooled by water. The 928 ought to have been wonderful – a smooth Aston Martin, but with reliability. But it never really appealed. The affordable 924 and derivatives, were uninteresting – 'PMPs'.

Being unstreetwise, I asked a girl: 'What's a PMP?'

'Poor man's Porsche,' came the answer. And terminal relegation for the product.

It is strange the way the factory has itself tried so often to close down the 911. Why? Did it get sick of it? It is so beautifully made, and so complex that the profit margins may have been too low. One more classic sent to the graveyard by the tyranny of the cost-accountant.

And yet, deeply regretful though I am at its parting, and immensely pleasurable it is from the moment you settle in the driving seat, it never quite, in my estimation, made the Top Four Great Drivers class.

Firmly in my reserve team are the Citroën ID; the Jaguar XK120 coupé; the Mercedes 300SL, and the very first Olds 88s.

My own choice for the nicest cars to drive – the indispensables – would be (and not necessarily in this order) the Bentley R-type Continental; the lightweight Silver Ghost; the

Citroën 2CV (circular headlights only) and the 356 cabriolet. All these cars actually talk to you, for most of the time, on a journey. The dear little 356 is slower in top than the 911 in fourth, and on a motorway now has quite a job holding off the Cavaliers, but every one of them is replete with personality. They used to get me down the Autostrada del Sole with the oil above boiling temperature the whole way, and be none the worse for it in the morning.

The 911 is almost too perfect; agile, obedient, incredibly fast, yet a certain amount of character has been lost. It is like having a conversation with someone on the telephone. With the 356, they're actually in the room.

Even so, I hope that my own car outlives me. Perhaps we'll go together. It is left-hand drive; and I tell my executors that on my tombstone should be written: 'He always went for the third lane.'

Some of the best classic cars to be had for under £10,000

In the November 1997 issue of Classic Cars, *the main feature looked at great classic cars priced under £10,000. Alan, of course, did not entirely agree with many of the cars selected and thought that a more challenging ceiling would be £5000. He felt that plenty of interesting classics could be had for not much money at all.*

He was probably being a mite optimistic citing a Jaguar XK140 Coupé as a contender. They are certainly worth more than £10,000 now, even in fixed head form. Alan's XK140 was one of his favourite road-going Jaguars. It was the fastest of the XK120, 140 and 150 range, apart from the exceptionally rare 150S with its 3.8 litre, triple-carburettor engine. Having lightened his XK140 by removing the bumpers, tweaking the suspension and relocating the battery, as well as fitting a few competition extras, he found it very 'nice and chuckable'.

Ten thousand pounds is really a lot of money and it can get you some nice pieces of machinery. Of course, every one has their own opinion, and such judgements are highly personalized. But I really don't think anything should be on this list unless it is fun to drive (ever had fun in an Amphicar, or a R080, or even a Silver Shadow?), or is utterly beautiful – or zany, or far out – to look at.

Myself, I would have put the entry threshold lower. If you have only spent £5000 on something, then you can enjoy it free of guilt. And this will still get you a 240Z (top of the list, in my view, for sheer durability and competitiveness – particularly with triple DCO carburettors and wide wheels), a Majestic Major or a very good Citroën ID (avoid DSs without a manual gearbox).

Anyone who was an impecunious student in the golden days of the breaker's yard finds it hard to accept that the decimal point has moved to the right – sometimes by as much as three spaces. In 1967 I bought a 3½ litre Bentley for £30. It was a Thrupp & Maberly close-coupled sports saloon with a trunk on the back, and I drove it, albeit hesitantly, sixty miles home. Four years later, I saved a DB4 which couldn't get an MoT, paying £450, and my sons, aged nine and eleven, learnt to drive in it in the grounds of Saltwood Castle.

After a bit, I sold the Bentley 3½ for £110 and the Aston, its suspension now non-existent, for £600. Carol Spagg bought the DB4, and left at once for a long French tour. But, as she ended up with the only type 158 Alfetta in private hands, she knew what she was doing.

The list is almost empty of American iron – unless you count the Mustang, overrated in my view; by 1966, US steel was already several gauges thinner, the doors didn't shut so well and the bodies rusted. The convertibles of the early 1950s are probably now too expensive for inclusion, but the two-door coupés, or the big wallowy woodies, will go on giving pleasure, invoice-free, for years. And the 1949 Oldsmobile 88, a Chevrolet with a 5 litre over-square V8 shoehorned in, is one of the top post-war greats. Try a skim through *Hemmings Motor News* rather than buying from one of the English dealers, who tend mainly to concentrate on the later cars with chrome and fins.

Some more omissions: the Austin A90 – the convertible was great fun, the styling archetypically 1950s. Surprisingly fast, all it needed were Konis and disc front brakes – anything will do; you can get them off a broken Golf.

And Allard; V8 only. The very sporty ones are out of sight, but a nice M-type drophead was sold the other day at an eligible price. And I would have thought, if one were careful and patient, £10,000 in cash would get you a 140 hard-top – cheapest (but fastest) of all the Jaguar XKs. The heart-breaking, bank-sundering, but heroic story of David Dalton's restoration of an XK150 coupé in last month's issue reminded me that the contemporary road test figures for the XK series were – XK120:

121 mph; 140: 129.5 mph; 150: 123.7 mph. The 140s were very good in club races too, and in their heyday some collected competition enhancements like close-ratio boxes and racing seats.

The most surprising omission from the list is the Mark VI Bentley. Best, and well under £10,000, are the really loose, well-worn examples. They will run for ever – particularly if your local MoT garage is understanding. But don't buy the first one you see. The variations are enormous, and comparative tyre-kicking is an essential prelude.

I always had a soft spot for the post-war Mercedes 180. With a sidevalve engine, but so beautifully built, even the horn-ring was solid instead of U-section. Better by far than a Peerless. But I suppose it all depends on whether you want to *drive*, or spend most of the time with Swarfega and a set of box spanners.

After the war many British cottage workshops foundered, and today there are only a handful left, producing specialist cars in small numbers

It's a strange irony that Britain produces the best mechanical engineers, but seems incapable of mass-producing decent motor cars. The hyper-competitive Formula 1 industry, as well as the top-end American race series, are entirely dominated by the British, yet Rover, TVR, Morgan and Bristol are the only remaining wholly-owned British manufacturers left. The Germans learnt to crack it with the Volkswagen Beetle.

Reading of TVR (I have never owned one but was sorely tempted, at Blackpool during the Conservative Party Conference, to slip over to the factory, three miles distant, and do some test driving) reminded me of how many brilliant little individual essays we've had on the post-war British car scene, and what their fate tells us.

In the 1940s there was practically no circuit racing, petrol was rationed and most 'sport' was mudplugging trials on very steep and awkward gradients, a kind of autocross in slow motion with only one competitor allowed at a time.

At first the Ford V8 was dominant, in Allard and Mercury Specials. Then smaller and more agile two-seaters with the lighter sidevalve four-cylinder Ford engines began to displace their bumbling cousins, Dellow being the most popular. As 'competition' vehicles became miniaturized, the old Austin Seven caught on; and it is worth recalling that the very first Lotus ever built had an Austin Seven engine, albeit polished, balanced and ported.

That little car, with its leather cockpit roll like an SE5a, hand-stitched by Hazel Chapman herself, was the first trials car to make the transition, on account of its durability and balance, to the world of club racing on aerodrome circuits. I well recall driving the first Lotus built for commercial sale, the Mark VI.

That was a real sensation. The Mark VI had T-type MG engines, bored out to 1466 cc, and was completely uncatchable up to 90 mph. Soon after, the Marx VIII appeared, with enveloping body and high (but functional) tailfins. And here again, when in the driving seat one had the sensation of crossing from one design era to the next. It was a deep divide, but spanned by barely eighteen months – from 1951, when Mike Hawthorn won every sports car race at Goodwood in a 1937 Riley, to 1952, when he did the same thing in a brand-new Cooper-Bristol.

Were they doomed, these brilliant cottage workshops? Having no wind tunnel, and being unable to afford the fee at the Motor Industry Research Association, Chapman and his team resorted to sticking hundreds of pieces of cotton fluff to the bodywork of the Mark VIII, then filming it at different speeds round Brands and noting the effect of the airflow.

And practically every component in the finished article, from engines and gearboxes to switches and steering wheels, was bought in. Only the brainpower of the young designers was unique. And their commitment. I once asked Colin Chapman what he really wanted, this before he had started on Grand Prix cars. 'To beat the Porsches on their home ground, the "Ring",' he replied. Much later, raising his sights, it was to win at Indianapolis.

In the end, sheer weight of 'working capital' got the whole lot. Peerless, JBM, Reliant (the Sabre, not the 'Nerdmobile'), Marcos, AC, Singer, Lea-Francis, Paramount (some of these were already brain-dead).

The sad truth is that once you get into making cars to *sell* you are prey to everything from cost-accountants – who hate quality – to corporation politics, where individual excellence is discouraged. But if you are making cars to *win*, then, thank goodness, it is different. Which is why we in Britain still conceive (I am trying to avoid the word 'assemble') the world's dominant Grand Prix cars.

At this year's London Motor Show there were few British

manufacturers, Rolls-Royce and Morgan being two. The B-pillar shutline on my 1996 Continental 'S' is 5.6 mm. On my old R-type with 'coachwork' by H.J. Mulliner it is 2.8 mm; on a modern Lexus the gap is less than 1.5 mm.

Meanwhile, each year the Morgan looks more like a replica of itself. This may be the result of compulsory crash-tests, or local licensing requirements in key markets. They no longer have the scale, or the purposeful grace, of early 4/4 models or the Plus Fours. And things have come to a pretty pass when one hears nostalgic talk of 'classic' versions of cars that are themselves sold as identikit classics.

The existence of an indigenous automobile capability is one of the main tests of a country's industrial strength. Whether we can rebuild ours is uncertain. It took only eight years for Germany to make the Beetle globally dominant, but they understood two initial requirements: total testing, and the need for a dealer network that stocks up on *every* spare part before it gets a single new car to sell.

In this kind of league, genius is not enough. Also required is attention to detail, and a sixteen-hour working day.

Saltwood

Sunday, 4 May 1974

Another weekend of total frustration, totally predictable pattern.

Down tired, but expectant and in good form, looking forward to release, playing with 'toys', etc. But cars wouldn't start – battery flat, jump leads useless, etc. Looked gloomily at cars at Ma Clarke's, all of which need cleaning badly (too depressed to go to Baileys where wrecked [Daimler?] waits, now in the open for a year with vandalized hood). Came back here and moved Cherrybum 3 litre to red garage.

To drive or not to drive your classic car during the dreaded winter months: that's the question

As winter draws to a close and classic cars are exhumed from garages up and down the country, owners are invariably faced with the same problem: old cars that are reluctant to start.

The Clark cars, kept garaged in various lock-ups and sheds in the grounds of Saltwood Castle, as well as around and about the local village, are not stored in ideal conditions. They are mostly dank and covered in damp dust sheets.

As is clear in this piece, Alan had a battery fixation, for which he was notorious in the motor trade. When he flogged a car, a young chap would arrive to collect it on a truck and when it was delivered to the London showroom, it was often found to be sans battery. Or, if there was a battery in the car, it was often a duff one that Alan had hastily charged up on his 'Loony Toons' charger just to keep it running long enough for the cheque to clear.

Once winter is upon us the pleasure – the need – of a classic car diminishes arithmetically as the bleak months accumulate; until at last, around the end of February, we lift the dust sheet. What do we find? I speak from personal experience, repeated year after year in spite of the best of resolutions.

The first and most obvious flaw in this preface is that there may not even *be* a dust sheet. Not spread over the car, at least, but scrubbed up in the corner of the shed, where it has been playing its part in the conservation of nature's cycle by functioning simultaneously as food store, dormitory and latrine for a small colony of mice.

Even if the car is sheeted you will find that – blast! – you forgot to turn off the battery master switch/disconnect the terminals. Amazingly, the ignition light does – just – glow a very soft red. It mocks you. Press the starter button and there will be a noise like a single blow on a tiny nail from a muffled hammer. And the red glow extinguishes itself.

Right. Battery charger. I have a special 'Loony Toons' charger on a trolley which, if in really vile mood, I can link up on 'boost' and operate the starter motor as the charge is going in. This is something you should only do if you are going to sell the car within the following few weeks, as it buckles the plates, wrecks the alternator, and burns out the leads.

So now – the idea of going for a little test drive rapidly losing credibility – carefully disconnect the leads, open the cells, top up with distilled water and allow the charge to 'trickle' in. Soon it's after lunch and the light is fading. A lovely day is changing to wind and drizzle. But we shall overcome. On the (highly optimistic) assumption that the battery will 'take' a charge, it still has tricks left to play. Notably a loud and irritating clicking noise when I (re)press the starter. I have been told that this is due to a 'bad earth'. Very occasionally, if the battery is really strong, one can get past it by holding, teeth gritted, the button in until the corrosion on the earth terminal post burns off. Usually all that happens is that the leads (again) get fearfully hot and all that precious charge so recently fed into the battery dissipates.

Next, having furiously cleaned up the terminals, you run into that second line of defence with which a classic electrical system obstructs anyone who actually wants to start the engine. Pump trouble. This is a special characteristic of that most loathsome of all accessories – the SU electric pump. Sometimes it won't tick at all; sometimes it does so sluggishly. Invariably, its performance is intermittent. A mild blow with a light hammer will occasionally galvanize it, but not for long. If the pumps are mounted on the bulkhead they can sometimes be reached as one drives along. I well remember a journey, bonnet open all the way, from Washington DC to Orange, West Virginia, in a Lagonda V12 and, by leaning out of the driver's window, tapping the pump with a jack handle every forty seconds or so.

What's all this in aid of? For most of the winter months B-roads in the South of England are covered with a strangely

This large red machine is a 1910 Locomobile, a terrifying experience to drive, not because it was fast, but because it had virtually non-existent brakes, which were only fitted to the back wheels. With massive chains driving the rear wheels, the Loco sounded tremendous and, thanks to its high seats, it offered great visibility so one could see the accident coming well ahead of impact. In this picture the car is being cleaned! It was being spruced up prior to sale, but Alan had second thoughts. He felt he had to own at least one chain-driven car, so he kept it.

Opposite top 'Little Silver' is the name Alan gave to his Porsche 911 Carrera Cabriolet which he collected new from the factory in Stuttgart in 1985. This was his everyday car and never once went wrong. Totally practical, it was the ideal unobtrusive super car capable of delivering formidable performance. Here the 150mph Porsche is parked next to the entrance to the undercroft wine cellar at Saltwood with its boot loaded with wine from M. Goisot's vineyard.

Opposite bottom A beautifully balanced, immensely fast go-kart, this 1957 Porsche 550A Spyder, which was Porsche-works driver von Frankenburg's own car, is incredibly light and agile to drive. Pictured here with its extreme pea-shooter racing exhaust pipe fitted, it has an odd 'crawler gear' for low-speed operation, but is only happy when really flying and the engine would rev seemingly for ever. 'Perhaps this is what a Bugatti would have been like if the patron had been building them in 1957,' said Alan.

Top The 1936 Buick Phaeton straight eight is kept on the Eriboll estate in Scotland where it is driven with the hood down as often as possible to savour the fresh air and enjoy the magnificent views. With its big and torquey engine, it chugs contentedly along the rough roads and trails with the effective heater keeping the passengers warm.

Inset Just past Altnaharra in Scotland, heading north to Eriboll for Christmas. Amid blizzard conditions the road disappeared resulting in the fully loaded Discovery going off piste. For long-distance travelling Alan regarded the diesel-powered Land-Rover Discovery as a better machine than his awesomely powerful Bentley Continental S. The economical Discovery would make up time while the fast but thirsty Bentley was filling up at yet another petrol station. Also, four-wheel drive helped rather a lot in these sort of conditions.

Left Alan trying to squeeze the Citroën 2CV into his father's garden house. On the Saltwood grounds cars are parked in every available shed, barn, outbuilding and garage and Alan even went so far as to buy a shop in the village because it had garaging for eight cars. No doubt his father would not have been amused at a Citroën 2CV in his entrance hall - it is hardly art.

Opposite top The Citroën was taken on one of the Hamilton Rallies, invitation-only events where entrants were obliged only to bring very special cars along. Alan was in his C-type Jaguar but when the weather turned foul he drove the back-up Citroën. Some entrants thought this was a bit off especially when the Citroën proved so fast over the difficult and bumpy roads they could not keep up. Alan had great fun blowing off a couple of supposedly very hairy Astons.

Opposite bottom Jane's lovely Citroën DS Decapotable was among the last constructed in 1973. One of only 1,365 ever built by specialist Henri Chapron it covered a very low mileage. The Clarks chose the paint colour and the cloth interior and even went to see it being put together in Paris. When it was finished Madame Chapron would not let Alan drive it away. As it was Jane's car she had to collect it herself. Alan, paying the cheque, was a little put out.

Below Grandson Albert behind the wheel of the little Citroën Mehari, Saltwood's mobile wheelbarrow, which being so light left no 'footprint' on the lawns; the rear section could take a good quantity of lawn clippings and compost.

Top The outrageous boy-racer Vanden Plas bodywork fitted to this huge 8-litre Bentley is actually original and not an Alan Clark special. First ordered by Captain Vivian Hewitt, the car features a cut-down windscreen, Le Mans instruments and lovely, very narrow fabric-covered bodywork. Alan paid a lot of money for this car but he did not keep it very long. It must have been the fastest lorry he had ever driven! Here it is seen attracting attention in Kensington Gardens at a Bentley Drivers' Club meeting.

Above James Clark at the wheel of the Scots Grey Bentley. The car comes from a famous Scottish collection and was painted battleship grey – hence the name. When it arrived at Saltwood Castle it was a 'non-runner', but James spent an hour with it and got it running.

Another motoring jaunt, here cars are stopped at 'Rest and be Thankful' during Charles Howard's AMG rally in July 1989. Alan's Jaguar SS 100 is second from left.

Seen here in white livery, this 1955 D-type Jaguar was later repainted black. The D-type, along with the Rolls-Royce Silver Ghost, are the two greatest road cars of all time, in Alan's opinion. The D-type is now owned by musician Nick Mason of Pink Floyd and Alan was happy that it is raced and well used. Nick Mason has done very little to the D and says, 'the car has no significant racing history other than a brief stint in Florida run by the original owner, a US army commander, the compensation was that the car was pretty well original. An added bonus was finding that all the numbers matched, meaning there would be no wrangling over its genealogy, and that virtually no restoration was required.'

Three Jaguars outside Saltwood: SS 100, SS 100 and XK 120. Alan always regretted selling his first SS 100 which he owned in 1946. He felt he should have kept it along with his XK 120 bought new in 1950. The car pictured in the centre was once owned by Mrs How, who ordered it from the Earl's Court Motor Show with special silver brightwork. The car embarrassed Alan once when it refused to start (Jane thinks it might have been in front of a woman he was trying to impress while filming a television programme at Brooklands). After that it was sold.

Not a fan of Italian cars in general and Ferraris in particular, Alan did however love this Ferrari 340MM coupé which he bitterly regretted not buying. This car, built for Ferrari racing ace Villoresi, was vicious, but it had real soul. Having witnessed two racing drivers killed in 340s, he accorded the highly strung thoroughbred a degree of respect. Really good Ferraris with the glorious Lampredi V12 engines 'could only have been built, and blessed, by the Italians'.

resilient slimy veneer. It's not exactly mud, but it's certainly not clear water. I have even quite inadvertently 'hung out', on a right-angled corner, the tail of a car built in 1910. Also, raindrops at 60 mph are incredibly painful. Spray and splatting from other vehicles runs down your neck. It's easy to see why 'tourers' became almost extinct in the 1930s and everyone wanted 'saloons'. If you don't fold the windscreen flat it will get covered in water on *both* surfaces. If closed, it will mist up in five minutes.

So my preference in winter is for bum-warmer seats, climate-control heating/ventilation, anti-lock braking and effective screen washers . . . As long as you don't allow yourself to be lulled into thinking that all is OK out there. A favourite manoeuvre is to 'join' motorways in the Bentley, using its 400 bhp in full. Mindful, of course, of Segrave's aphorism that if you are always going faster than anything else no one can run into you from behind. (As he also recommended crossing intersections at top speed in order to minimize time in the danger area, one can understand why he died at thirty-four.) Not long ago, the slip (*sic*) road being covered in slime, I did find myself occupying both inner lanes at forty-five degrees on full lock, though still enjoying Segrave's immunity. Winter should be a time for discretion, summer for display. That, after all, is nature's own rule.

Saltwood

Sunday, 11 May 1975

And here is my own life, its ['serious'?], ambitions, political and however-you-like-to-call-it side so emphatically biased by those experiences, well over halfway through, even deducting the childhood years. I've got ten – *tennish* – more years active, eight as an 'active buffer', the remainder as a sage. That's always assuming freedom/deliverance from the screech of brakes, sickening thud and rending of metal from the head-on crash over the brow of the hill. Now that the 550A Spyder is roadable I often take it out on fine evenings. So intoxicatingly fast and agile – but so vulnerable. Going on to the slightly blind humpback of the A20 Sandling Bridge I visualized (as so often) that horrid impact. Have I recorded that nightmare spin in the 230SL that night when I was unscathed? Let us hope it means that 'what is written, is written'.

The current Porsche Boxster cannot match the 550A and the best interior belongs to a Land-Rover Discovery

This issue of Classic Cars *focused on the best classic motor car interiors and Alan had to provide his alternative twist – the Land-Rover Discovery.*

The same issue featured a Porsche 550A and the then new Boxster, which was being touted as the modern version of the diminutive Porsche racer of the 1950s. The 550 won the epic road-race, the Targa Florio, was fourth at the Nurburgring in 1956 and was driven by such greats as Stirling Moss, Jo Bonnier and Taffy Von Trips. As Alan rightly points out, the Boxster is not even in the same league as this pure-bred racer with its fabulously alive responses. The modern Porsche, professing to be an exciting sports car, is sadly numbed down, like all cars today.

Allow me to record my own enthusiasm, derived from long personal experience, for the Porsche 550A and the unwelcome (for the connoisseur) conclusions to be drawn from comparison with the Boxster.

The tiny 550 was the most perfectly balanced and responsive of all post-war sports-racing cars. It is what Ettore Bugatti would have been making had he been in his prime in 1955: smoother and quicker than the OSCAs, less brutish than the twelve-cylinder Ferraris, less demanding than the 750 Monza, and less quirky than the D-type. There is still nothing quite like a 'D' on really smooth surfaces but, under pressure, potholes, drain covers and bad camber make it really hard work – which is why Mike Hawthorn's performance against the 300 SLRs at the Dundrod TT in 1955 ranks as one of the great heroic drives of all time.

The little 550, though, besides having the sweetest engine, is quite unperturbed by bad surfaces. With its very short wheelbase it handles like a modern Grand Prix car. Changes of attitude should be avoided at all times; and better to scrub a bit off the front than let the tail go, because when that happens it is impossible to get it back and the next thing is a heavy 'goodnight'.

Throughout the three years of my ownership, I never touched the engine except to keep the (dry) sump oil fresh. I bought for £3000, sold for £7000 – groan, groan. Those were the days when one often took a margin simply so as to convince a mildly disapproving family that what appeared to be a self-indulgent hobby was also profitable. So it may seem strange that one of my principal reservations was the car's *fragility*. The slender gearstick, drilled pedals, the delightful 'nervousness', as the French call it, of all the machinery did sometimes make me wonder, when I was really piling it on, what I could do if it broke. This is not a feeling that you will ever experience in, say, a Cadillac-engined J2 Allard.

Nor do I believe that this would ever occur to anyone trying to get the most out of a Boxster. But the contrast between the two Porsches exemplifies what transpires when an autocrat is supplanted by a design 'team'. It also happened, and over the same period, to Ferrari after Enzo began to decline from his prime and Lampredi no longer designed the engines. The car is conceived around the table by a group of people whose principal purpose is to advance their careers by scoring points off each other: not just accountants, but sales directors, 'fashion consultants', and nerds with tables of data from consumer surveys.

There is a mutual conspiracy to isolate driver from machine. Every device, from rubber bushes to tiny servos, assisting such diverse functions as seat adjustment and climate control, increases the weight and desensitizes the responses.

Where today is the workshop that will make a rapier of Toledo steel, a Purdey twelve-bore like they were in 1932? A work of art so perfect that the customers will pay – and that needs no *marketing*.

This nostalgic gripe has left me little space for the very important topic of interiors. These have to be considered within the context of driving and movement, and there are two schools, the first of which teaches that for maximum satisfaction you should be held tightly in your seat.

I'm not so sure. The high driving position and big, wool-upholstered bench seats of US cars of the 1950s can offer the most comfortable and, because you can sprawl about and keep shifting your position, one of the most tireless ways of covering great distances. My dear old Land-Rover Discovery TDI still gives the best compromise between the two, as you sit high and seem to have stacks of room. Do remember though, as I have often warned and for which corroboration regularly accumulates, that the handling of these cars – and steel-sprung Range Rovers – becomes dangerous at over 80 mph.

There are a number of detailed practical considerations which no one bothers to address. It's often hard to find the switch for auxiliary foglights – so important on motorways and only needed when you can't take time off to look at the dash. And when are the Euro-busybodies going to standardize windscreen wiper operation? How many times have you deftly signalled a right turn across fast-approaching traffic, only to be startled by wiper blades frenziedly scraping a dry screen?

On arduous motorways the tortoise can be faster than the hare

In this issue of Car *magazine, which featured British cars and a distinctly British theme, Alan argues that his Land-Rover Discovery is an almost ideal vehicle for the long journey to his Scottish hideaway in Eriboll. With its diesel engine, the Discovery uses less fuel than many much faster machines and therefore spends less time at motorway service stations. Apart from its British Leyland standards of build quality and some nasty cheap fittings, the Discovery has, surprisingly, proved very reliable.*

What makes a car distinctively British? A lovely smell, I suppose, particularly from the posh ones. You notice it as soon as you open the door, and it can last for almost a year if you don't smoke inside. Otherwise, it's all bad.

Total unreliability – no peace of mind whatsoever. Weak shock absorbers, uncomfortable gearboxes, dodgy electrics. Ultra-downmarket quality of minor components – bolts, brackets, jubilee clips that seem to have been fabricated by the inmates of an Overseas Development Agency hostel in Mozambique. And those ill-thought-out secondary controls: handles and switches, and nil-output horns and heaters.

Sometimes you get all these characteristics in one vehicle – the Allegro, for instance. Sometimes, mercifully, only about half of them. But throw in general and accumulating indications of poor assembly, and indifferent inspection procedures, and it is all too easy to see why there aren't any British cars left. The death of the native British motor industry is the longest, most damaging and most expensive act of industrial suicide since World War Two.

So it is particularly ironic that practically the last completely British vehicle produced should be not only the best, but also the cause of the final extinction of the company that made it. Not because (like, say, the 8 litre Bentley) it was so expensive, but because it was so good.

Even today, after owning one for two years, I find it hard to accept just how much the Discovery will do, and how painlessly. It will carry five people quite comfortably, and masses of luggage. It will accommodate enormous loads with the rear seats flat. It will run all day at 90 mph, and in its high, high fifth gear it will creep up to 100 mph helped by wind or gradient and still not over-rev.

Incredibly, you cannot get the fuel consumption below 26 mpg, and under 'normal' conditions it will give well over 30 mpg. Often, we have covered 500 miles on one tankful. And therein lies an illustrative tale. It is 578 miles from Saltwood to Gleneagles – our first stop on the long drive to northern Sutherland. The whole journey, excepting the first five minutes from Saltwood to the M20, is twin-track or motorway. In the Continental 'R', travelling at 115 mph (and more wherever possible), we make three fuel stops. In the Discovery, at a steady 90 mph, just one. All too often, the tortoise will arrive at its destination before the hare.

Another key merit: the Discovery has *never* gone wrong. Among its stablemates, only the 911 (bought new in 1985) can match this record. Indeed, with the exception of a somewhat lethargic heating system (apparently remedied in the 1994 car), the Discovery accords perfectly with the three principal requirements of the motor car:

(1) It must *invariably* start.
(2) The interior must get warm well before you have got the children to school.
(3) It must be *totally* reliable.

Never mind colour, trim, shape, styling or even performance. These are the three fundamental criteria. And if you're really honest, you'd be amazed at how few cars can satisfy them. My

1950 Chevrolet Club Coupé can – even now – but there aren't many others.

Faults inherent in the Discovery? The only one I can think of is the rear door. It's huge and cumbrous, won't always stay open, and sometimes jams shut. Just a little touch of nostalgia, to remind you of BL 'workmanship'.

And as with all good machinery, there is the temptation to abuse it beyond its design limits. The Discovery, with its high driving position and spacious cabin, is wonderful over great distances. But it is not a GT car. Long, long curves (stretches of the A9 such as, say, descending off Drumochter summit towards Inverness) can induce a curious and unwelcome corkscrewing motion at 85 mph. Driving rain, thickish traffic, worn wiper blades, someone pulling out to overtake the Shore Porters Society artic in the left-hand lane – and you have all the ingredients for a through-the-Armco spectacular.

The heart of the vehicle is that wonderful direct-injection engine, a turbocharged diesel of – for its size and weight – prodigious torque. It must rank with the original long-stroke twin-cam XK engine as one of the finest internal-combustion units ever made in this country. And it is the shape of the power curve, together with better suspension than any competitor, that accounts for its terrific off-road performance. Peat, sand, snow: it will cope with the lot. Because under 'normal' (non-Blomqvist) conditions, torque is more important than power. The Discovery is happy to change up at 6, 11, 17 and 28 mph – like an Alvis Stalwart – if you like that sort of thing.

And now, I suppose, all this is going to end. BMW has a very high opinion of itself as an engine designer (not shared by me, I may say; I prefer Mercedes for strength and Lexus for sophistication) and will presumably want to insert some show-off unit with four valves per cylinder and peak power at 6200 rpm. No doubt BMW will seek out the moron who some months ago tried to substitute a 2 litre petrol engine for the TDi, and put him in charge of production engineering.

BMC – or whatever you like to call it now – has always been riven by corporate rivalries and factionalism. For most of its life the volume-rubbish (spelt 'car') division has been pillaging the four-wheel-drive balance sheet to conceal its own shortcomings.

The sales success of the Discovery was purely consumer-demand led. Management never marketed it properly, first putting resources into the doomed Sterling campaign (only a genius could consider naming a product after a commodity that was always being devalued) and then trying to get people to buy Vogues instead of Land-Rovers. The Discovery simply sailed along on that strongest of all tides: word-of-mouth rec-ommendation.

My own car is two years old, and I am going to turn it in for a new one in September – provided the specification hasn't altered. That would be my advice to you, too. Buy now while stocks last.

If the weather's too bad for driving, get lost between the pages of a good book

In the depths of winter it's difficult to come up with a decent subject, as classic cars are locked up and the weather is miserable.

Alan chose to focus on good books, giving a personal account of the ones he liked, usually ones that included his cars.

On the assumption that most of you (in Britain at any rate) will read this issue on a day when the weather makes driving – or at least *viciously* driving – a classic too difficult, I am going to write about books. There are some incredible books around. And for the price of a set of tyres, you can get a small library of fascinating reading.

Beware the 'coffee-table' volume, though; huge, replete with illustrations we have all seen many times, and written in a kind of 'cor-look-wot-she'll-do-squire' style that is irritating for real classic enthusiasts and connoisseurs.

Top of any list has to be Morgan and Wheatley on *The Restoration of Vintage and Thoroughbred Cars* (Batsford). This seminal work was first published in 1957, when Silver Ghost engines were in breakers' yards being stripped of their copper for melting down. It's written with wit and enlightenment in abundance. Of pre-war Concours d'Elégance they comment: 'It was always the practice for entries to be presented by fashionably-dressed society beauties. It being understood, of course, that the judges would not subject these ladies to the same level of scrutiny in order to verify age and condition.'

Most of the really absorbing books are both specialized and full of *lists*. They are what is known in the fine art world as *catalogues raisonnées*. As a military and political historian, I know the critical importance of contemporary data. I practically never throw away a 'car mag' and at the top of my house there is a room completely stuffed with ancient copies of *Autocar, Motor* (in its heyday with Laurence Pomeroy and D.B. Tubbs – the best of the lot), *Road & Track, Mechanix Illustrated* and *Sports Car,* the club magazine of the SCCA (Sports Car Club of America) in the 1950s. Here, forty years on, I was able to find a picture of the C-type (013) which I presently own, competing in Nebraska before its very long (but fortunately dry) hibernation. Pre-war issues of *Motor Sport* are also a superb fount of pictorial information on the early history of interesting cars. If you buy one at a jumble sale, make sure the small ads are all there. To my horror, whilst researching old *Autocar* magazines at Iliffe bookshop, I found that some nerd had vandalized all the ads at the back 'in the interest of more economical storage'.

Of the major works, it's a tie between Karl Ludvigsen's *Mercedes-Benz – Quicksilver Century,* which contains over 600 pages and thousands of photographs illuminated by a really erudite text, and Fasal and Goodman (twin volumes in a slipcase) on *The Edwardian Rolls-Royce.*

Ludvigsen's book gives a wonderful impression of Mercedes' invincibility (pre-elk test, of course). It pictures the car that I would most like to own (I believe it no longer exists?) – Caracciola's *Bergkampf* special SSK.

John Fasal gives a special quality to his book by confining the illustrations to contemporary photographs. Both of these works take at least a week to read and can be browsed forever after.

Johnnie Green's *Bentley, 50 Years of the Marque* was the dominant reference work for many years, and second-hand copies can be expensive. The book has now been superseded by Michael Hay's comprehensive listing of all the 'WO' cars, and Michael Ellman-Brown's book, which does the same for Derbys. In the former, I was pleased to see my own 3 litre described as 'last heard of in 1959 – present whereabouts unknown'.

With Jaguar, there is of course an abundance of potboilers, so beware. The latest major work, *Jaguar Sports Racing Cars,* by Philip Porter (Bay View) is essential. Its two predecessors, by Paul Skilleter and Bernard Viart (both Haynes), are also compulsive reading. My own personal favourite remains the elusive tome of Terry McGrath, *The XK in Australia*. It includes lots of illustrations that other publishers might have banned on grounds of 'taste'. Read this and no longer can you be excused for not knowing what your C-type, D-type or XK will look like after hitting an electricity pylon, or bouncing off three other cars, or doing half a lap (as it must have seemed) on your car's roof and then waiting for the fire brigade to arrive.

Another excellent book is John Reynolds' *Original Citroën DS*, which should be read – if your French is up to it – with Olivier de Serres' *DS Le Grand Livre*. Predictably, the most interesting books are about cars that arouse the highest affection. Which is why I am surprised that I know of nothing top-class on the 356. Any recommendations?

Finally, there are books written in personal reminiscence mode – Stanley Sedgwick, Rivers Fletcher et al. They are fun to read – once. Having said that, my favourite articles in *Motor Sport* were in the *Cars I Have Owned* series. And one day I intend to write my own version.

The romance of the motoring mascot

Not only was Alan keen on car books, he also had a love of motoring mascots. Over the years he added a number of very important mascots to his collection but seems to have disposed of most of the really good ones, much to his regret. In typical style, he likes his mascots to be original, ones that have actually experienced the open road at the end of a bonnet.

When Tutankhamun's tomb was opened, pride of place among the countless treasures therein was held by the sun-crested falcon, mounted on the Pharaoh's chariot to guide him on his journey to the other world. And for three thousand years man has adorned his vehicles, from ships to sleighs, with emblems cast in his own image, or that of animals that he loved or feared, all intended to give that vehicle good fortune and a special, personal identity.

Now that motor cars are mundane and uniform, and excrescences are prohibited by law, many owners try to achieve the same effect with 'cherished' number plates. But in the days when motoring was difficult, exciting and a privilege of the few – its Golden Age – there flourished a special art form, the mascot, or *bouchon de radiateur*. This is rapidly becoming a major collectors' field, and so the appearance of a definitive reference book[*] is timely. It gives us an opportunity to offer some guidance on pitfalls, taste and (because, like the cars themselves, it is already infested with hoarders, dealers, 'investors' and general fakers-up) on values.

[*] *Car Mascots: an Enthusiast's Guide* by Giuseppe di Sirignano & [David] Sulzberger (Macdonald & Jane's: 1977).

127

And let me say right away that I have nothing against such people. If you are going to have a free market there are bound to be a lot of parasites who give it momentum. I have no patience with enthusiasts who complain because someone else's 'greed' prevents them buying a 30/98 for £245. As I (and presumably every reader of this paper) would like to buy one at that figure, the only way of deciding who actually gets it is to put the price up until there is only one person left who will pay!

What we *can* do is exercise our own intelligence and discrimination. Most dealers are quite stupid; they don't (with certain notable exceptions) know their subject in depth and they tend to be highly conformist, all trying to buy the same thing at the same time. If this is true of the cars it will be even truer of the mascots, where errors often start even in the auctioneers' sales catalogues.

Messrs di Sirignano and Sulzberger (whose photographs on the dustjacket with their R-type Continentals may, or may not, increase your confidence in their judgement) have laid some excellent groundwork. They rightly classify mascots into three main categories – Custom, Fantasy and Proprietary.

Custom mascots were executed for rich motorists from 1908 until the slump of 1929, usually by distinguished artists and sculptors of the art nouveau and, latterly, the Cubist movement. Very small runs were made, and were always signed in the foundry by the artist. Sometimes only a single example was created, like the Cobra specially forged for Valentino's Knight-engined Voisin, and the naked girl running from her bathtub – why? perhaps she heard the phone ringing – on Gary Cooper's Duesenberg.

For the connoisseur, dating is critical, and highly important to value. Valentino's *actual* cobra, assuming its provenance could be established, would be enormously valuable – say, £2000–£3000 – and Gary Cooper's girl not much less. But the Cobra was copied twice; in 1927 all the Isotta-Fraschini 'A's that went to the United States (twenty? twenty-five?) offered it as an option, and a second version, reduced in size and chromed, was available over the counter in the late 1930s. The Isotta version is worth about £375, the 'commercial' not much more than £90.

So take care! Size and signature are the key, as some dealers on the Continent strip the chrome off 1930s reproductions by a process of reverse electrolysis. Gary Cooper's girl also had a short run in the late 1920s (all signed 'Joe Descomps') but was thought too sensuous for the middle classes and never appeared in chromium plate. A bronze or silver-plated one – practically impossible to find – could be as much as £600.

A number of other special creations of the Custom period were later bought and patented by commercial firms like Desmo, and Beard of Cheltenham, and were mass-produced with chromium finish for sale to the wider motoring public of the 1930s. Invariably, however, much of the quality of definition was lost, and they were sometimes reduced in scale as well. Two well-known examples are the 'Speed Nymph' (later adopted by Lejeune as a trademark), which was exquisite in the original bronze, and the erotic 'La Sorcière'. Genuine ones from the early 1920s are worth over £300, the mass-produced versions £65– £85. However, I do remember buying an original one at a Christie's sale in South Kensington where it was offered in the catalogue as 'and another', being coupled with a rather ordinary Beard 'Kiwi', so it is always possible to pull something from under the combined noses of the dealers and auction staff!

Really there is scope for a full-scale work simply on this Custom, or bronze-age, period. One would like to know more of the leading artists – Bazin, Le Verrier, Martel, Bofill – details of the foundry runs, which designs were commissioned for whom and so forth. One Le Verrier girl, a coked-up flapper doing the Charleston, used to be offered on early Delage D8 chassis. Some research into the catalogues of the various *concours de bouchon de radiateur*, and the prizewinners, would be helpful.

Moving on into the age of Fantasy, one is amazed by the variety produced in that last decade before the war. Not only the quality but the theme ran from top art deco to low-grade kitsch. There is the orthodox – horses, dogs, jockeys, golfers, huntsmen, girls of course in profusion – although by now *style* is suppressing sex (not always successfully though; take a look at no. 57, 'lizard standing on a rock'). Also much whimsy – different kinds of gnome, caricatures of policemen, dolls and monkeys and a loathsome little mechanic called 'Speedy' (the original of D.B. Tubbs's 'Oliver Bash'?). One of my own favourites, the Schneider Trophy seaplane, is not illustrated. Like a fool I sold my only example some years ago and have been trying to find one ever since.

A guide to values in this section is impracticable – but without set market patterns it should still be possible, with taste and persistence, to build up specialized and valuable collections. Interesting (and genuine) chrome mascots of the 1930s command between £70 and £120 in the saleroom. Beware, though, the crisp and newly minted! Some popular pre-war lines are being reproduced. Put the two examples side by side and the differences in quality are immediately noticeable.

I myself would never buy a reproduction, although they tend to make up over half the content of auction entries. In this connection the authors sometimes display a certain naivety, as 'Old Bill was England's favourite cartoon figure during the Great War, there were many mascots of him ...' (there were not all that many, in fact, but the crudeness of definition and bulky shape makes him very easy to fake in modern moulds, and no auction is complete without its complement of brand-new brass renderings, often with metal drip still on the moustache) '... and today one occasionally sees him on the hood of cars in England, showing that the owner is a veteran of the Great War' (!).

The stars of this period, carrying on the artistic tradition of the Custom years, are the Lalique constellation. Fragile and impractical – the risk of theft or vandalism makes it virtually impossible to leave one unattended on the bonnet of a car today – their beautiful and opaque lustre has always attracted the attention of collectors, many of whom probably don't even know how to drive, and can still less call themselves 'enthusiasts'. The result is that one cannot get one of the larger pieces for under £300 and some of the rarer items (like the Greyhound, or the orgasmic 'Vitesse' trophy) would be over £500.

As one reflects on the wide demand for Lalique in the antique trade (incidentally both the authors of this book are antique dealers, like so many vintage enthusiasts, thus illustrating the interplay of aesthetic and mechanical appreciation that underpins the movement), one should remember this useful tip. Early bronze and silver-plated mascots were often removed from the cars when the owners sold them, and were mounted on wooden stands. In the present confused state of the market the auctioneers seem to follow a rule of thumb; if it's on a radiator cap, put it in a mascot sale; if it's on a stand, put it in a sale of 'The Decorative Arts'. At the latter, prices *may* with a bit of luck be substantially lower.

Finally the authors discuss, quite systematically, the field of company mascots. Here demand is largely regulated by the collector's need to restore his favourite to total originality – although some mascots, particularly Guynemer storks and 'Flying Ladies', are collected independently, with a corresponding inflation of their values. I well remember when, as a penniless student on holiday in Cannes in the early 1950s, the taxi rank on the Croisette consisted of a row of Hispano-Suiza H6Bs with Landaulet coachwork (mainly by Castagna or Kellner), all somewhat down in the mouth – the more prosperous taximen favoured those ugly Peugeots with headlights behind the radiator grille – but each one worth over £20,000 today.

Each Hispano carried a perfect stork on the bonnet, and I went down the rank buying them for 10,000 (old) francs each, or about £9, until my money ran out. When I got back to England I sold them all, not having the sense even to keep one back, and paid for the holiday. Today an original stork is very expensive – up to £400 with the beak intact – so beware of replicas. Shallow but unworn (i.e. unpolished down the years) wing lines are the easiest give-away.

The authors make some mistakes of fact – they are weak on categorizing the different Bentley mascots and, for example, omit the angle change with the introduction of the MR series in 1938 – but this section is a good general guide, and reminds one of long-extinct makes whose emblems were works of art in their own right. What about the Beck (of 1920–22), whose bonnet bore the 'Vertige de la Vitesse': 'an apparently terrified girl holding her face in her hands and trying to keep her balance against an onrush of wind'.

Can I end with an expression of personal preference? To be worth acquiring, *a mascot must have been on a car*. It must have lanced through driving rain and sleet on the Route Napoléon; stood patiently in the baking sun of the Riviera, strained to vanquish some rival emblem in long and perilous dices down poplar-lined roads. To this extent they share the mystique of coin-collecting. If they could but speak, and tell of their mounts in the past, and of the rise and fall and even death of those through whose hands they passed ... And to this extent they share the mystique of vintage machinery – that they must be awakened from time to time, and placed on your radiator, and allowed to relive the joys of *élan* and *vitesse*.

Dean's Yard

Tuesday, 27 May 1975

After two days very successful openings, fired by the cash flow, the possibilities. One of the few 'enterprises' unlikely to be troubled even by the envy, the jealousies all around us. I also have these romantic fantasies of the besieged aristocracy. 1791. I do hope the boys will catch on in the end. James in particular is unbelievably idle about it at the moment. He has passed through girls (for the moment) and drink (largely speaking) and now is obsessed by driving. He had cleaned the Bang Bang meticulously during 'garage invigilation' on the public days. Last night Tuppy suddenly cocked an ear and said, 'That's the Bang Bang engine ...' I looked out of the door and saw it going down the drive – James was turning it prior to putting it in the garage. I waited in the shadow of the Barbican. The car came back, turned in the car park gate and then out back down the drive! I knew what would follow and sure enough an engine opened up (so like an aero engine it sounds) and the lights clearly shone charging up Sandy Lane! I got the Land-Rover, but by then he was already returning. Oh dear, I do love 'Boy' so much, in spite of all his bolshiness of growing up. I do dread his having a motor accident. I must train and nurture him on the road. He wants to go to Lydden★ and one might do that.

★ Motor-racing track off the A2 north–west of Dover.

Like other Specials, Triumph's minimalist TR2 is basic but terrific fun to drive

A step on from his favourite Q-cars is Alan's Bentley R-type Continental Special, known as the Bang Bang. While he expresses a love of American hotrods, his special is a blue-blood machine, a true one-off, as James Clark explains in his Introduction to this book. He told me he thought the car was jinxed, because it had killed in the past and, on one occasion, James was driving it through the grounds of Saltwood and very nearly ran over his grandfather.

The 2 litre engine Standard made in the early 1950s was a good tough unit. Four cylinders, overhead valves, nice wide bores so plenty of piston area – along with the immortal XK and the F-head Bentleys and Rovers, it was one of the very few completely new designs that the British motor industry produced after the war. Standard had conceived an excellent car – the *Vanguard* – to sweep the markets which were starved of dollars and short of gas. Unfortunately, and typically, it was badly assembled and the telescopic shock absorbers were filled (or so it seemed) with a mixture of glue and waste paper.

But the engine went on to power the Triumph Roadster and was bought by Morgan for the Plus Four. The Triumph was really nice and the coachwork beautifully made. It was a *touring* car, not a sports car, spoilt only by the absence of an overdrive, while the 1952 Morgan was, in my opinion at least, the best car ever to come out of Malvern. Not as fast, obviously, as the V8s, but more compact and better balanced.

The success of the Plus Four gave Standard an idea: why not make our own sports car? Not in an old-fashioned chassis like the Morgan but with modern IRS and a very short wheelbase. Whether it was visionary or (more likely, given the congenital piggy boardroom resistance to any project of this kind) improvisation, Standard decided to shoehorn the 2 litre engine into the 850 cc Standard Eight.

The Eight was an ugly and broadly useless 'rival' to the Morris Minor, but it was no heavyweight and, with a skimpy two-seater body, weighed even less. This solution – the Triumph TR2 – really worked. I never owned a TR2 and I must admit every time I drove one I felt slightly unsafe (in contrast to my feelings as a passenger, when I was almost constantly white-knuckled with apprehension). But it really got around, performing well in long-distance rallies, like the Tulip and the Alpine.

The TR2 is a good example of a factory-built 'special': that is, the result of looking round the store cupboard, bolting various components together and (a great feature of all 'specialist' manufacturers) letting your customers do the development work. Contrast, though, what Porsche was doing at the same time. The early 356s were equally dangerous, perhaps more so in inexperienced hands. But every piece of the chassis, drivetrain and bodywork complemented the other, giving perpetual driver satisfaction.

The big-engine-in-light-chassis avenue is the preferred route for the exciting Special. But remember just one – very broad-brush – design rule. If the springs are hard, the chassis must be flexible; if the chassis is rigid, then the springs should be soft. Ignore this and you will either bounce, or wallow, off into the landscape.

This was a mistake the early US hot rodders made. Putting those torquey flat-head V8s into Model A roadsters made them incredible in a straight line – until something, even a ripple in the concrete, would cause the steering to 'wander'. Even so, an original Mercury-engined hot rod with ¾-race and ported heads is one of the nicest fair-weather, medium-distance drives you can find.

In any case, isn't part of the fun of the hairy Special suddenly getting into a *crikey!* situation as the hill, or the circuit, catches you out?

In bygone days I made such a Special myself, and it still languishes in the innermost recess of an unlit shed. In 1961, when a good Bentley Continental was not worth much over £1000, I bought an insurance write-off (chassis 65 D in case the BDC historians are reading this). I sold the remains of the body, shortened the chassis and stuck on a *very* skimpy aluminium body.

How and why it held the road as well as it did remains a mystery to this day, particularly as it is on Wraith wheels so as to still further raise the gearing. That was/is the most incredible car. It will start easily from standstill in top gear, or do 120 mph in third. But really, of course, this Bentley is no more than a four-wheel bike, in the tradition of the Shelsley Specials of the 1920s and 1930s or even earlier, when 1000 cc JAP or Vincent HRD twins were latched on to children's cots, or even wooden frames, and can be seen in those sepia Lartigue photographs, scorching around the long drives of the great country houses.

Today there must be lots of good Japanese bike engines in scrapyards; why not revisit some of those crazy Specials? Remember, though – thin wheels.

Recalling his greatest drive of all reminds Alan of his longest love affair with his Jaguar XK120

Alan is in full passion mode here, relating the best drives of his life. He was much more than simply a classic car enthusiast – he was a driver who relished long runs across Britain and the Continent in wild and raucous machines. His wife, Jane, recently looking at a photograph of a young Alan and his beloved XK120, well remembers him courting her when he was driving it.

Everyone will have their list of truly memorable drives, when machine and circumstance were in perfect harmony. They remain fixed in the mind, and the car concerned will hold its place in the personal pantheon of favourites. If I list mine (in descending order, but very closely bunched) they would be the following.

First, the lightweight Silver Ghost on the penultimate day of the great Alpine Rally, crossing the Gaberlsattel Pass, on 4 July 1993.

Second, my first drive in a D-type. It was an early short-nose production car, with wrap-round cowl and headrest (no fin). I can't recall the chassis, but its registration was KDB 100. Pure low flying – but without nav-sat software. I would arrive at traffic intersections, mini incidents, at 120–130 mph. I was 'delivering' it for a friend in time for practising at Silverstone on 6 May 1956; from Shepherds Bush, about an hour and a half (no motorways). Another thirty minutes and I think St Christopher would have felt obliged to withdraw his protection. The car was an aborted Italian order, and so painted scarlet. Years later I heard a 'restorer' boasting how he had 'got it back to the original BRG'.

Next, my first night drive, over the Cotswolds from Burford, in a one-week-old Bentley Mark VI. There was no traffic then, in 1947, and for the first time (also) I was listening to Tchaikovsky's *Capriccio Italien* on the radio. Steering, brakes, gearshift and power were all in balance like nothing I had ever experienced before.

Then, another Jaguar. Sir James Scott-Douglas let me 'try' his Ecosse C-type. I was still only a student and when I brought it back, ticking, full of delight at having mastered (as I claimed) getting it to drift on full power, he didn't seem too pleased.

And last, but not least, the ex-Villoresi Ferrari 340 MM. *So* wicked. I have written about it recently, so will only send this message: 'My love, where are you? We must meet again . . .'

Looking at this list I am surprised that my longest *affair* of all doesn't get a mention. Perhaps because we did it so many times. But I do remember the exquisite, heart-in-mouth gentleness with which I drove home my own Jaguar XK120, bought new from City Motors in Oxford – I still have both the sales invoice and the car – on 18 November 1950.

The margin possessed by a 120 over other traffic was quite incredible. Rather like a 911 Carrera today, only the bikes could give it a run. The Vincent Shadow was the hardest to overtake, but the Triumph Tiger 100 could give trouble too.

In those days the XK never seemed to overheat; they all do now. Jaguar's Competition Department prepared it for the 1953 Carrera Panamericana, using many of the mods that had gone into the C-types that dominated that year's Le Mans. I think she must be practically the only 120 with *Dunlop* disc brakes. It also had many other enhancements that became optional later on – close-ratio gears, heavy torsion bars, 2 in. sand-cast SUs, 70-gallon tank with baffles, and much else.

Sadly though (I know better now, and always retain and store original fittings), the sweet and smooth engine whose number (W2014/7) is still engraved on the chassis plate was, I assume, pulled to pieces in the factory. Now she has an un-numbered fourteen-stud blue-top head with a 9:1 compression, but never seems as silky (or is it just nostalgia?) as in her heyday on dish wheels (you can still see the grooves for the spats on the rear wings) with a 3.27 ENV axle.

During the 1920s, and for a good while into the next decade, a Cricklewood Bentley was *the* British sports car. Drive one today, though, and it feels like a Massey Ferguson 6/90 – except slower off the mark. But the XK engine went on winning races for almost twice as long, first in the XKs, then the Cs, then the Ds. Then it dominated production car racing in the Mark II, the Coombs version of which remains to this day one of the nicest ways of getting from A to B.

The other day I was at a breaker's fire sale. There, standing in the rain, was row upon row of Jaguar twin-cam engines, lifted from crashed or rusted 'donors'. What were they making? Forty pounds, sometimes as much as £60 . . .

One owner from new: a lifetime spent with a white Jaguar XK120, an 'Open Sesame with the girls'

Alan owned his Jaguar XK120 for close on fifty years. As he says elsewhere, he was probably the only person left, with his own hair and teeth, to still own a 120 he had bought new.

As the European Correspondent of Road & Track *magazine, he used the Jaguar to tour around Europe, ostensibly following race meetings in the vein of D.S.J., the famous Denis 'Jenks' Jenkinson of* Motor Sport *magazine. Although Alan stuck at it for a while, he did not have the staying power of Jenks.*

In 1959 he bought a later model XK150S, which he did not like, and the E-type Jaguar that followed was even less pleasing.

This article was for Jaguar World *magazine but Alan remained honest and critical about the different Jaguar models without resorting to any diplomacy.*

One of the (many) sad things about life which one realizes as one grows older is that the intensity of feeling, particularly of pleasure, diminishes with age. I don't think this is true of physical pleasures, eating, etc. (especially etc.), but it is certainly valid for intellectual ones. The most intense sensation that I can personally recall was getting a black 2½ litre '100', at the age of seventeen, in 1946 (I spun it on the way home at the junction of Fitzjohns Avenue and Swiss Cottage – but that is another story). Second, without doubt, was gloating over its successor in November 1950 in the showrooms of City Motors in Oxford – where I was an undergraduate – and knowing that after a brief period 'on exhibition' it was going to be mine. In those days the XK120 was a good five years ahead of *any* other sports car and was totally unobtainable on the home market.

On the road it was sensational; silky smooth with an absolutely even power graph and an enormous margin of performance over anything one was likely to meet. Those were the days of the 'ton up' kids on Triumph Thunderbirds and Vincent Rapides (I suppose their descendants are driving Mini Coopers? One hardly ever sees a big bike these days) and I remember some fabulous dices along the North Circular, or down the A20 as far as Swanley, especially after I fitted dual exhausts and a 3.27 axle which gave over 70 in second. The brakes never gave me any trouble but they, and the suspension, needed a bit of reinforcement for racing. The car got on to the leader page of *Autocar* clouting the oil drums at Boreham while lying third. You had to get them as hard as nails to be any good at circuit racing, and have courage as well. I reverted to boy-racer, howling up the Kings Road at night and lifting my foot in third to hear that beautiful musical burble on the overrun. I used to get cast-off Dunlop racing covers from Mac at Albany Street – the old diamond pattern in those days – which made a delightful whine on certain road surfaces.

For the winter of 1951–2 I had attached myself to a ballet company (for personal reasons) and was living in Monte Carlo. It seemed to be the only XK in the Principality and made (I don't doubt) a pretty mixed impression carving round the streets at all hours with three and sometimes four dancers squeezed into the front seat. Coming up the hill from the harbour you could just peak in second before braking for the Hôtel de Paris right-angle. I recall meeting Prince Bira, quite by chance; he was driving a very early MG (M-type?) in his personal shade of blue. Even then it looked very old-fashioned. It was, he told me, his very first car and he sometimes took it out for fun. I felt a pang of nostalgia for the '100' but resolved, at least, never to part with the XK.

In 1952 my evident idleness, forced – quite understandably – my parents into draconian measures. I was reading for the Bar and was very short of money. The XK sometimes got into the Inner Temple and raspingly sharpened up the lawyers' aural senses; more often I made the journey by bus. Soon, however, I was earning pocket money from a new American magazine –

Road & Track – which I had bamboozled into appointing me European Correspondent, and got mobile again. I took off for the Continent, doing a sort of poor man's 'D.S.J.' and getting to most of the major circuits. 1953 was the swan-song of the XK in its original form. She did an enormous mileage, going down to Hyères for the twelve hours' race, then up to Le Mans where she was the last car to go round the circuit before the start – I was testing the traps past the Hippodrome café and the Omega certificate I have shows 212 kph, not bad for a 7:1 compression engine and soft cams! Forrest Lycett and Laurence Pomeroy both drove the car at this time; I remember having a wild ride in the latter's modified Mark I Ford Zephyr trying to keep up with my own car.

Then in the late summer I finally got the OK from *Road & Track* to do the Carrera Panamericana, and talked 'Lofty' England into modifying the car for me. The factory did a tremendous job: special engine with a light flywheel, cylinder head, cams, big carburettors; a short-shafted competition gearbox with wonderfully close ratios, a multitude of chassis improvements, clutch, torsion bars, rear springs, and a forty-gallon fuel tank. I have an invoice for these, as indeed I have for every piece of work ever done on the car, and it covers pages. Originally Jaguar were going to enter a C-type made of heavier section tubing (that car was subsequently sold to Duncan Hamilton) and when that entry fell through they really went to town on my car. This made it all the worse when I, too, chickened out.

The following year I took it to Italy. I recall a drive to Ferrari and a crazy demonstration drive in a 3 litre Monza driven by Sighnolfi (he was later killed doing just that). The XK was tremendously fast now, and I remember leaving the factory at Maranello one evening behind Ascari in a prototype, unpainted, 4.4 litre six-cylinder, and going up to Abetone. I was trying like mad, he – to start with at least – was relatively leisurely. After about thirty miles he had around half a minute on me; I would be burning the brakes out downhill on to the bridges while the silver Ferrari was climbing up, about fifteen *lacets* away, into the pine trees of those endless bleak Alpine valleys. But by half-distance to Florence I had lost him completely.

In 1955 a minor miracle took place and I qualified as a barrister. There was a last fling in Italy, then a positively last one on the English beaches (it was a record dry summer) until late September. A white 120 was still an Open Sesame with the girls then, and the car was back to its old Monte Carlo form of howling along the sea front, late-night bathing parties and so on – a good deal less strenuous than keeping up with Ascari in the Appennines! This was the car's last year in continuous use. I had bought a VW for The Serious Life and, except for some more beach work the following year, it went into retirement. It didn't emerge at all in 1957, 1958 or 1959 (or if it did it wasn't taxed!). Marriage took place in 1958 but did not force sale. In fact we honeymooned in the VW.

In 1959 I bought a new 150S roadster, in red. The 120 had a narrow shave, as I was offered £350 in part exchange – a very good price in those days. Thank God I stalled for a bit until I had got used to the 150. It was soon apparent that it didn't have half the character, besides being impossible to drive fast without one's hair, scarf, tie or whatever being blown backwards and fiendishly into one's face. The *coup de grâce* was administered on the Hurstbourne Tarrant–Andover road when I was overtaken *suddenly* (at 85 mph you don't expect to be overtaken suddenly) by a green, heavily modified 120 hardtop. I did my best but couldn't match his performance, and this confirmed what I had already suspected – that the heavier 150 just did not have the speed and agility of my Mexico car. Nor did it make the same delicious music. Not long afterwards the arrival of the Stork excused the sale of the 150 and its place was taken by a Bentley Continental, which I still have.

In 1960 I had the car out for a short while and let Dick Protheroe carry out certain additional modifications to the engine. At the same time disc brakes and sixty-spoke (but original diameter) wheels were fitted. At this date I took out the seats (which I retain) and fitted two Jaguar racing bucket seats. In every other respect the car looks original, including the chrome on the grille and sidelights which, although nearly twenty years old, look perfect.

Looking at the service log I see that the XK did 52,000 miles prior to the 'Mexico' conversion; about 12,000 in 'Mexico' form, and only 3000 miles in the past ten years (i.e. since being 'Protheroe'd'). I have had no trouble with rust, probably because at the time of the Mexico conversion the body was completely disassembled and the underside and mating surfaces scraped off and rubberized. Since virtually every moving part was renewed by the factory competitions department in 1953 the effective wear on the chassis in its present form is only 15,000 miles – and it feels like it, wonderfully solid.

I have tried the E-type twice, in 3.8 and 4.2 litre form but they never won my heart the way the old 120 did, and once Jaguars ceased to be independent, much of my old loyalty faded.

If original is best, why are highly modified classics taking all the Historic Rally silverware?

The fact that a Willys Jeep won the 1997 Peking–Paris Historic Rally really annoyed Alan. As he points out, the drive must have been pure purgatory but on these regularity runs the average speed is set at 30 or 40 mph, which the Jeep could just about manage. This win was a victory for dogged perseverance rather dashing motoring style, which somewhat misses the point of the grand tour...

What do we want a classic car for? Showing off, of course. Nothing wrong with that; they are more idiosyncratic than beach jewellery. Most people enjoy staging their own mini-concours in the pub car park. But the real fun is driving them, on long journeys, at high touring speeds and, preferably, on unfrequented roads.

It is twenty-five years ago this month that I had a 'race' (illegal) for a wager (doubly illegal) with my old friend, the dealer Charles Howard, from Calais to Mike Poborowski's villa in the South of France. I was driving a four-wheel-braked Ghost, fitted by Jonathan Harley with a brilliant twin (Rolls-Royce) carburettor conversion for running in the 1973 Alpine Commemorative Rally.

It was amazingly fast in the middle range, although the fuel *supply* system had not been altered. Thus it could not provide for the appetite of the carburettors; and the driving technique was not unlike early turbo-equipped cars, like the Saab 99, or the first Quattros, where for maximum surge effect you had, for much of the time, to be on brake and accelerator pedals simultaneously. Charles was driving a Hispano HB6 which was rumoured to have a Monza engine. First to arrive got his petrol for nothing, and a heavy lump sum in cash.

In fact the Ghost 'won' (having led up until that moment) when on the second day the Hispano melted its exhaust gasket. But the whole experience was tremendous fun, redolent of the great intercity races of pre-war years and quite hard to replicate in 1998 – or at least not on *routes nationales*, which are now too crowded.

This was not so much a long-distance rally as a private duel, but of a kind that can often come about on such rallies. Now the calendar is congested with such events. Some are thinly disguised races on public roads; others are set up for Regularity jaunts. Others are just scenic, and gastronomic – little chance of a dice, unless one or more of the competitors has consumed too much white burgundy at lunch.

The trouble with the first two categories is that they are becoming too competitive. Or rather that the drive to victory through modification will, if not strictly regulated, soon make the winning cars unrecognizable as well as highly disagreeable to regard or to ride in.

The rally in which I would most like to have driven is the Peking–Paris – an incredible saga, curiously under-reported even in the specialist press. But I do think that it was outrageous to allow a Jeep to win. No one drives a Jeep for more than sixty miles for pleasure; only with gritted teeth to get (for example) to the Remegen bridge before it's blown up.

Classic rally organizers should be much stricter about enforcing eligibility. They should remember Fangio's first great triumph in the 1940s Gran Premio del Norte, three times across the Andes in a Chevrolet; Marcel Becquart, unbeatable in the 1950s in his Hotchkiss; Böhringer dominating the early 1960s in a Mercedes 220. One of the last great road-races and a model for classic rallies today was the 1950 Mexican Carrera, won by an Olds 88. Every car was a 'stock' sedan. The Italians sent an Alfa team led by Villoresi but they couldn't keep up. Soon the sports-racing cars took over, with huge support teams of mechanics and spares. A few years ago it was won by a *replica* of a real C-type.

Am I being a fogey? It's the fat tyre syndrome. Classics look dreadful on low-profile rubber. I'd go further and say that they shouldn't really race on aerodromes at all. The imposed stresses and the driving techniques are of a completely different order than at, say, the Ring, or Donington, or even Brands. But the runway culture has now pervaded the sport to such an extent that if you try to run a genuinely standard car at even a VSCC event you become an object of pity and derision. I see the risk of this invading the whole field of classic rallying, with the leading cars turning into loony-tune gutted roll-cells straight out of a forest special stage. Look what's happened to the Californian Baja.

But I admit that I can't wait to get into another really good rally.

What car will I use? The 911 is too low and cooped up for a long period. And I need at least 60 cubic feet of space for casks of still mineral water. The Citroën DS23 Decap remains firm favourite for anything not too rugged.

For the highest attainment, I keep in my garage, untouched, the ideal vehicle for the Tibetan plateau – a 1950 Chevrolet coupé. Ultra-low mileage, so no incipient stress fractures. High, strong and comfy. All it needs is a set of Konis, 7.00 tyres, a sump and tank guard, an oversize radiator, a gearbox oil cooler and an auxiliary fuel tank.

None of these modifications will even be detectable by a spectator. That's the way I like to be. It's the Q-car complex.

Saltwood

Friday, 24 November 1978

Some shoulder pain and *cold hand*, but this morning a fabulous experience. Flew again with James, in the little 150 as one climbed high over Rye I could see Rye Harbour, the little boats, and the garage that used to be the 'Big' garden, and then we climbed high – into the clouds, a range of strato-cumulus like 'over Italy' from Trockener Steg. Fantastic beautiful moving experience as great cloud valleys rushed past and towering cliffs loomed over us . . . To think that my son, whom I used to kiss goodnight in his cot in that little room, was now piloting me in this fairyland.

On the way back, my mind miles away, James suddenly said/shouted, 'Daddy, what are you doing!' and I rammed some cheeky red-coloured but new Peugeot 104 from behind; seconds later a Yank in a blue Ford ran into us! And what's more I'm in the Chapron!!! Setback. It must go back to Chapron, that's all. Darling Jane took it very calmly, but I was shattered – old person accident – also wondered about whether I might have aggravated my 'whiplash' injury.

Classics are made for summer but watch carefully for signs of bad behaviour

This is an amusing summary of driving in perfect weather, again displaying Alan's keen understanding of mechanical things. He's right to assert that carburettors work best on cool summer nights when the air is dense and moist.

And with all historic and classic cars, perceptive drivers keep a constant eye on the gauges. Unlike modern models, older ones are very sensitive to the conditions and need constant monitoring – 'Classics are like horses ... do not ride them too far without rest or water.' That's why we like them: they respond to intuitive driver involvement.

I have written in the past about the huge difference the weather can make to classic motoring. Of course snow, old-style 'Monte' conditions, is great fun. Dress up in that Bomber Command 1943 flying suit (or better still, if you can get one, US 8th Air Force, Schweinfurt Raid), take spade, torch and thermos, and enjoy yourself.

But rain, wind and fog are different. They make the whole thing purgatory. You may think that you can get around in (say) an E-type coupé. But the demister and the wipers don't really work properly, do they? Personally I'd rather be in anything Japanese, however miniature, than a Bentley S1 – until, that is, you hit the slewing Transit broadside on. Now, at last, we are in early summer; reminded of how a quite small difference in the ambient temperature – from say 58° to 63°F – makes the whole difference to open-top motoring. And a time of year when, at dusk, those traces of ground mist seem to make twin SUs run so sweetly.

All my great drives in classics seem to have been in early June, when the hours of daylight are so long and, in the far north, blend into the dawn. I remember as a student trying to get to Glen Brittle in the Cuillin Hills in one day from Hampstead, being determined to climb Sligachan over the weekend and return. I was in the SS, and took the last ferry across to Skye in broad daylight at 10 p.m. That last stretch I was so exhausted that I never once changed gear nor, I am ashamed to say, did I drive much on the left. My black box would have recorded eighteen hours without, in those days, a single mile of motorway.

But it is in conditions such as these that you grow as one with your mount. Every beat of the exhaust and creak of the bodywork is part of the romantic experience: something you will never capture in a Volvo wagon. Classics are like horses, they will always be faithful, but do not ride them too far without rest and water.

And little signs, equivalent to the movement of a horse's ears, can be a good indicator of mood. One of my least favourite is water-gauge ratchet. The coolant temperature steadily rises. Heavy traffic or a long hill and it will look menacing. But each time that you get an opportunity to cool it down – slipping into neutral on a long descent, or whatever – the gauge never quite goes back to where it started. It establishes what financial markets call 'a new floor'. Then a more disturbing symptom intrudes – gauge surge. One moment it's at 60°. Winter cruising. Then suddenly it's at 90. Tightly cornering a small roundabout and it's back to 70. Soon the last stage – gauge euphoria. The dial reads zero.

Stop at once – because that's also the amount of water left in the radiator.

Do you also find, in July and August, the pedals get very hot? It's heat transference, of course. But not a very good sign even if, like me, you enjoy driving in bare feet. Not long ago at some posh dinner I sat next to a beautiful woman who inflicted on me one of the best motoring put-downs I have ever suffered . . .

She told me how in her youth she had loved, best of anything at all, a Bentley 4½ litre.* Bought from Jack Bond for £130

* Corrected here (Alan had called it a 4 litre), as a subsequent 'Back Fire' article admits.

during the Suez War forty years ago. It had been 'cut' and lowered, and would do the ton.

Patronizingly, I asked if she had ever mastered changing gear without the clutch . . .

'Without the clutch? One summer was so hot that I drove the whole way from Falmouth to Anglesea (a beautiful route of some 170 miles across the Welsh Marches) without touching the pedals, and kept my feet cool by hanging them over the side.'

Try it some time.

Before signing off I must apologize to a correspondent, and all who noticed, and were irritated by my inexcusably muddling the monocoque Standard Eight of the 1950s and the neat little pre/post-war Eight which had a real chassis frame, and which formed the basis of the TR2. The other question, also raised on the letters page, as to how 'new' were the F-head Rolls engines, is more open to argument. The B80 was the first, and the last, straight eight ever to be made by Rolls-Royce. It transformed the Mark V Bentley into the 'Scalded Cat', but corporate policy never allowed it to be used for what God had intended – an implant into the R-type Continental. This would have created a classic in the same category as the Bugatti 57S, or the sports-bodied Mercedes 38/250. An example, of which there are all too many, of the boardroom losing its nerve at the last moment.

Recollections of driving a Jaguar SS100, an experience steeped in nostalgia

The Jaguar SS100 was Alan's second car, replacing a rather large 6½ litre Bentley. As he explains here for the Daily Telegraph, *he did a number of epic drives in the SS. Most people would baulk at the thought of driving from London to Skye in a modern car today, let alone in an open 1936 model Jaguar.*

The SS100 is the most *obviously* charismatic of all the sports cars built in the 1930s and 1940s. It has a long, louvred bonnet, huge headlights with built-in mesh covers to protect the lenses from stones thrown up by vehicles you are pursuing in the Alps, and a snarling exhaust note. Add to this acceleration that still allows the driver to mix it aggressively in modern traffic and a simple, understressed engine that is completely reliable and you have the perfect toy for a rich, but slightly retarded, male . . .

I have had one in the garage for nearly my entire motoring life. At one point, when they were very cheap, I had two (the car being auctioned by Robert Brooks is not my 'real' car, which features in the *Diaries* and presently reposes in a shed at Saltwood, but the 'support' version, which I hardly ever used).

I've never actually taken a driving test. At the end of the war there was some kind of procedure whereby you could get a provisional licence with a demob certificate and then after a bit it got upgraded. I was long on theory, short on practical experience. As far as I was concerned there were two positions for the clutch – in, or out. I mean, either the engine was connected to the transmission, or it wasn't. This made manoeuvring in confined spaces, such as the garage of my parents' house in Hampstead, somewhat *abrupt*. And they were relieved when I substituted the SS for my first car, a 1926 6½ litre Bentley weighing nearly three tons, which I had bought for £325 on long-leave from the 1946 summer half at Eton.

Another little knack that I mastered by experimentation was going round corners in the wet. The SS was not, repeat not, the same as the old Bentley in this kind of situation. Indeed, on the way home to north London from buying it (opening that very day an overdraft with the Clydesdale Bank, an admirable institution with which I don't think I have ever been in credit since), I accelerated firmly and confidently on the rain-sodden woodblocks, which at that time formed the road surface where Fitzjohns Avenue branches off from the Finchley Road. The car spun right round. Passers-by cheered. This was generous of them. All I can say is that I've never spun a car since, not right through three hundred and sixty degrees anyway.

A little later when I was more, as I thought, accomplished, I learnt about the front-wheel skid. The road was bone-dry, but I was going far too fast: tight corner, granite wall, hub gouges, king-pins shear, tense flesh strikes brittle aero-screen – as Ted Hughes might put it.

God was certainly kind in those days, just as He was, thirty years later, to my sons. And if anyone is thinking *He should have been punished*, well, he was: I lay awake until the small hours night after night, waiting for my children's return, knowing exactly how over-confidence and the need to show off causes young people to drive idiotically, no matter how fervent and well grounded is the advice given to them by their elders.

In my own youth I undertook some epic drives in the SS. Once in June I motored to Skye from London in a day, helped by the midnight sun. But I was then so exhausted that I slept round the clock and missed the only opportunity to get round to Coruisk in fine weather (an expedition I have still not accomplished).

I took her to Portugal and 'left the road' as the climax to a long duel with some locals in a new (1948) American Ford.

They very sportingly stopped and towed me out of the ditch. American cars were boss in those days, particularly the big Chryslers, and the Lincoln-Zephyrs with Columbia axles, which could absolutely sing away from the Jaguar on long hills. I did, however, once have a fabulous race with Nubar Gulbenkian, from Estoril to Sintra. He was in the back of a chauffeur-driven Buick Super, with the hood down and a very ornamental lady by his side. The chauffeur wasn't really up to it and I expect the wind, in every sense, affected the passengers. Anyway we almost dead-heated to the cathedral square in Sintra, where I posed for a photograph.

While I was an undergraduate I kept the car in the Morris Garages, a long tunnel of a place with a glass roof (it was formerly stabling, I would think, and is now demolished), for 7/6d (that's 38p) per week. Undergraduates were not allowed cars until their last year, so I just spent the evenings polishing. That paintwork must have taken more coats of beeswax than a Louis XV commode. But sometimes, late at night, I would run the risk of driving out on to the Witney straight where in still air you could get a speedometer reading of 100 mph. Not another vehicle in sight and the great headlights cleaving the darkness. Very Dornford Yates. And the precursor of hot July evenings thirty years later, when I used to drive back from the House of Commons with the windscreen flat after a late Division.

One of the delights of the SS is that it is still very competitive. Ian Appleyard was winning Alpine cups with it, against far more exotic machinery, even in the 1940s. But I won't 'strip' it, or change to thick wheels, or commit any other of the acts of vandalism that are necessary to win in VSCC events. Even untouched and untuned, the SS is still quick enough up hills to disconcert the fanatics. When Jane and I went on the AGM Rally in Scotland in 1989, the SS was the fastest pre-war car up the long Rest-and-be-Thankful hill climb and was only beaten overall by a Mercedes 300SL.

I don't know if the SS is my favourite drive. It would be a close thing. But it is steeped in nostalgia. Whenever I climb into the seat, memories rise at random from the subconscious, probably because nothing on it has changed – seats, colour, smell, the relationship of all the secondary controls, sound, responses. It is the nearest thing I have to a Time Machine – for going backwards.

Saltwood

Sunday, 26 November 1972

Gloomily contemplating collapsing looks and physique; derelict sex-life; continuing state of flux on field hence total standstill on such things as decorating, improving, protecting Saltwood. Purchase of the great 38/250 ex Malcolm Campbell, a most important car, means must rationalize down to eight in the collection, plus a few favourites (such as the XK) plus trading oddments. Can get by with a bit of scratching, sell about 20,000 [pounds'] worth of cars, possibly Woodfall. Still a whole list of the outgoings: the shop for little Mrs Clarke, various bills on cars, overdrafts. Only consolation, Zermatt almost eliminated so V-sign to UBS★ at last; they even have security somewhat diminished by expiring of permits etc. Thinking of death, disease, famine and bankers' orders.

★ Union Bank Suisse, which had loaned money to AC to build the Clarks' Zermatt chalet.

Money – is that all we give a fig about? Try having some fun with your classic cars

Alan again exhibits his catholic tastes when it comes to cars. He's not constrained by fashion or social pressure. Yes, he has owned some of the most highly regarded 'greats' but he has also had a lot of fun in more mundane machines.

Car writers are obsessed with sensation – line, speed, handling, show-off factor, and, not least, value. But if I look back through the cars I have owned, those that are memorable are ones that I held in deep affection. Some of them are 'greats'; three of these I am lucky still to own. But let me just pay my respects to three others that gave me some thrills.

The first (I guarantee no reader will have anticipated this) was a 1953 Vauxhall Velox. This little four-door saloon only weighed 18 cwt (the later cars with 'spinner' front were much heavier). It had a six-cylinder engine of 2.3 litres and a three-speed gearbox, bench front seat and pleasing, upright driving position. In London traffic it was almost unbeatable; in the countryside very hard for far more expensive machinery to shake off, even though the maximum was only a tick over 80 mph.

It was yet another example of a dreary car transformed by an engine transplant – the original offering, called the 'Wyvern' had a gutless four-cylinder motor of 1½ litres. Then someone decided to drop in a Bedford truck engine as an 'option' – and 'hey presto'. Is there one left anywhere, I wonder? If you find a Velox in the garage of a little old lady who has recently passed away, don't hesitate – just call me.

Next, a faithful 2CV, bought new in 1963 and collected in Lyons. Suicide doors, round headlights and total peace of mind.

Whenever I drive it I recall the philosopher Diogenes, who disclaimed material possessions, and a famous victory over a Ferrari 250 on icy roads in the Jura.

And lastly, my very first Beetle, the 'Standard' model in field grey, without chrome and having a 'crash' gearbox. Once the Michelin 'X' tyre arrived you could make a Beetle do anything. And there is one other characteristic of these three cars that made me love them. They never, under any circumstances, gave the slightest mechanical trouble.

So, you see, value isn't everything. It can be a comfort (if it's going up); an anxiety if diminishing; and is nearly always an unwanted inhibition on crazy driving. But it is not necessarily an indicator of behind-the-wheel enjoyment.

At the Goodwood Festival of Speed last month I saw GP 10, the magnificent Mercedes 38/250 which I owned in the early 1970s. When I restored it, I took immense care to paint magnolia on every nut and bolt on the white-enamelled chassis frame before reinserting. This, to a connoisseur, would indicate total disassembly before restoration. But I noticed that whoever last restored the car had simply sprayed everything the same colour, so that from some angles the great beast looked like a giant fridge.

I also noticed that its manner of going was just as belchingly hesitant, as after I had written the last cheque on the restorer's bill. A reminder of Clark's Law, which decrees that the more important and historic a car, the more sparing should be the restoration.

I suppose that with its long competition history (it was bought originally by Malcolm Campbell) this Mercedes must be worth getting on for £1.5 million. But it is the only car, including the first XK120S, in which I have completely run out of brakes (unusual with mechanical actuation).

In 1973, I sold it for £38,000 and thought how clever I had been. But today, as then, I guess I could keep up with it in the 2CV; and would have got past in the sweet little 'Standard' VW. The jolly Velox would have been uncatchable.

Finally, apologies to all Bentley enthusiasts for a typo in last month's column. The car driven by the beautiful barefooted girl who never touched the pedals between Falmouth and Anglesey (see page 150) was a 4½ litre (of course); not its dreary and unreliable economy-class successor, the '4 litre'. As Bentleys came designated in the engine sizes of 3, 3½, 4, 4½ litres, mastering the specification can be a muddled business.

We spend too long in modern cars. Classic cars could – and should – be used every day

When Alan suggests that 'car writers are obsessed with sensation – line, speed, handling, show-off factor and, not least, value,' he should also have added that we (classic car writers, admittedly) are obsessed with what the future classics will be. As he points out, cars have changed over time but the rate of change has slowed. Not only that, modern cars are produced in huge numbers, are full of complicated electronics that cannot be fixed with a screwdriver and have emission plumbing with a sell-by date. With the exception of a few ground-breaking machines, most moderns just become old cars and, as he says, 'After that, it's so what?'

When the Vintage Sports Car Cub started up in the 1930s, its nucleus was a group of enthusiasts who would meet at the Phoenix pub near Hartley Wintney. Their theme was that the cars being made in the 1930s were not as much fun to drive, nor as well built, as those of the earlier decade.

The Great Slump of 1929 and the recession that followed marked the dividing line. After that the cost accountant was king, and hidden 'savings' on every aspect of manufacture – durability of metals, size of components, gauge of steel in bodywork – made their intrusion into every aspect of the manu-facturing process. Add to that the 'horse-power tax', plus the fact that most people had suffered a mood change with the economic climate and wanted tiny engines and (as the customer didn't like shifting gear) even lower final drive ratios.

Recognize any of these factors today?

We cherish our classics for a lot of reasons – the camaraderie of those who share our taste; the fun of showing off; the pleasure of relating to vehicles that are still recognizable as machinery.

But do we drive them? Not much. How many readers of this column actually drive to and from work in a classic car? But the founder members of the VSCC used their cars all the time. It practically got you blackballed from the club if you were seen driving anything built after 1930.

Of course it is true that modern cars are much more convenient. They start, their interiors get warm quickly and (if built in Germany or Japan) they don't go wrong. But, in fact, the pace of development has slowed right down. And the customer has just become a giant milch cow for the motor trade.

If I look at my own garage I can see this point most graphically illustrated. In the far left corner is a very stark, very battered 3 litre Bentley, made in 1926. Twenty years earlier, cars as we know them didn't exist at all. They belched, spluttered, shook; and you had to light the acetylene headlights with a match . . .

But next to the 3 litre sits a Rolls-built 4¼. Only ten years on, very refined, elegant, and just as durable. Another twenty years (including the war, when from 1939 to 1946 no cars were built at all) and there is a Bentley Continental. Even softer in the mouth, beautifully built, and good for 115 mph or 20 mpg at a constant 70.

Then you have to fast-forward forty years to reach the last one in the row, a 1996 Continental 'S'. And what's the difference? Better 'climate control', and improved stability in a straight line. That's about it.

In other words, for the whole of its second cycle, motor car development has yielded very little – excepting a handful of really outstanding cars like the Audi Quattro, or the very first Golf GTIs – that is recognizably better all round. Spotting 'classics of the future' is a mug's game – if only because the authors are usually far too generous and often try to plug their own cars. I would add the Saab 99 to the GTI and the Quattro, possibly the first Mustang convertible with a stick shift, the 240Z, and the first Subaru. After that, it's so what?

Some of the very best and usable cars I have ever owned were ordinary saloons built at the end of the first fifty-year cycle. I have already mentioned the dear Velox (see page 157). I would give anything for a new version of my 1950 Oldsmobile 88, in which I put up several still-unbroken A to B records. And the best of all, a 1962 Mercedes 220, bought new from the factory.

I was writing *Barbarossa* at the time and told the Works I was taking the car across the Crimea to the Caucasus. It had an armoured sump, a special battery and heavy-duty springs and shocks. It was the most durable-feeling machine I have ever owned. I part-exchanged it for the Mercedes 600 (a bad car) in Switzerland and recall with a pang the dealer who gave it a road test. He turned to me in surprise after just two kilometres and said: 'Very good hold-roading.'

But where is it now? Working as a taxi in Zurich, I suppose. It most certainly won't have worn out.

Some say that a passion for classic cars is a sign of a mid-life crisis. Take that as a compliment

Alan enjoyed driving a wide assortment of cars for several decades. He once again highlights the pleasures of 'driving' and experiencing the feeling of life in a car rather than just posing. In reality, he was a very sophisticated poseur who truly enjoyed winding people up with his ratty-looking cars. On one of the Silver Ghost Alpine Runs he overheard a gauche but rich American comment that if Alan could not afford to maintain a Rolls-Royce properly, he should not be allowed to enter the event. Alan's inverted snobbery went into overdrive!

Twenty-five years ago, when the first issue of *Classic Cars* hit the news-stands, the 'movement', as we now call it, was in a very uncertain condition. I wasn't even an MP but driving around in a Citroën Safari filled with baby gear and waiting for the endorsements to drop off the edge of my driving licence. For amusement, I tore about in a Bentley 3½ VdP, £450 worth, in which I had won a club race at Silverstone a couple of years before. I think I must have been mad then (a view now confined mainly to wives and girlfriends). I mean, what about spares? Why was I throwing my money away, etc, etc?

Well, in 1972, I bought a D-type for £4000 and an R-type Bentley Continental for £1300. These two cars and the 3½ have appreciated exponentially; the decimal point has moved along to the right – two stops. But quite a lot of stuff, highly thought of at the time, has barely kept up with inflation – and certainly not with the FTSE or the Dow Jones Index.

Try shifting this week a Riley RME or a Corvette. In most cases, it'll be 'nice car but not really interested, old boy'. The great blue chip of the period, the Duesenberg SJ, is still expensive but what brokers call 'very narrowly bid'. And Rolls-Royce, the make that got the whole craze started, are on the whole – Silver Ghosts excepted – low-expectancy items at an auction.

I welcome this. Because as the movement spreads and its base widens, a quite resilient sense of quality and taste is asserting itself.

Of course those coming new to the scene and full of enthusiasm will make mistakes, come to dislike their choice and then not care to admit it or cut the loss. But in essence, this is a market that becomes more sophisticated with each season that passes. There now seems to be a growing recognition, for example, of a truth I have been arguing for years that overly 'restoring' historic machines and ironing out their little quirks and blemishes is a kind of vandalism.

There is also a growing preference for driving quality – fun or precision – over beach cruising and pulling power. If you want to know which side you're on, ask yourself this question. What would you rather have for the same money – a hot Frog-eye Sprite or a Triumph Stag? An Aurelia GT Coupé or a Ford Thunderbird?

There are a few commentators around (usually drawn from that same pool of busybodies who want everyone to travel by public transport) who will say the whole thing is one giant symptom of the male mid-life crisis. So speaking as someone who has been enduring (enjoying, you could say) this crisis for the last thirty years, I'd retort, 'Long may it continue.'

Because of the crisis I have so many favourite drives to look back on. The lightweight Ghost in which I ran the great Alpine commemorative is still at the top of the list. But I often think second place should go to a Porsche 356B Super, which I no longer own. I took it all the way down to Crete and back in the summer of 1962, never once putting up the top. That car would go round the clock, to 120 mph – yet return almost 40 mpg if you drove gently. I know that there are modern cars – particularly the high-speed turbo-diesels – that will do this today, but none feel alive in the same way as that little red Porsche.

A strange characteristic in a machine, this feeling of life. I still have three Jaguars: my original 120 roadster, the C-type and an orphan 140 hardtop. Now, the 140 was bought as a rolling spares bank for the C-type because it carried a lot of 1950s factory mods – racing seats, high-compression engine, heavy torion bars, close-ratio gearbox and other things. But every time I get into this car, shut the door, start the engine, I feel so at ease. It never stalls or misses, vibrates or boils or smokes.

Why I should prefer it (an admission that can only be whispered) to the other two is most mysterious. Perhaps the 140 is like a 'rescue' dog. Having been abused, beaten and revved to death on club circuits all over Britain (and in Australia too) it now knows that it has come home and is loved.

Supercars are expensive garbage which attract too much attention

*Flashy pose-mobiles are once again dismissed in favour of
Mercedes with big engines and no badges – real Q-cars.
Superbikes are a thrill, as was the Porsche 550A. Ever aware of
the market value and the real cost of owning million-pound
supercars, Alan suggests a selection that would keep the
enthusiastic driver both happy and solvent.*

A marvellous book has landed on my desk. Called *The Story of
the Supercar*, it's a guide to the classics of the future. Some of
today's classics, like the DBS Vantage, the Miura and the
Daytona, have their place, the photographs and the assessments
at the end are brilliant, but (is it a sign of age?) after a bit I put
the book down and thought, *I don't really want any of this garbage.*

I'd quite like to try a McLaren F1, but some of the stuff –
GT40, XJ220, Testarossa – I'd actually pay not to have to ride
in. There is a brilliant description by Ian Fraser of a mad drive
with one of the Ferrari testers who spoke no English and
mistook, through the cacophony, a pleading '*basta*' (enough) for
the injunction 'faster'. Fraser twice tried, and failed, to climb
out of the car, a quite nasty Mondial Quattrovalvole, before the
demo was finished.

In his introduction to the book, John Simister says: 'You're
never alone with a supercar. Wherever you park, someone will
engage you in conversation.' Quite, I totally understand my Swiss
and German friends who drive those special Brabus-converted
Mercedes with 6.7 litre engines, massive brakes and suspension –
and all identity badges except the three-pointed star removed.

These cars do have performance, of course, usually beyond

the limits of exploitation possessed by the majority of pop stars, Forex dealers and cocaine smugglers who make up their clientele. But most of them are still too heavy, and all of them are too low on the ground really to enjoy a long-range high-speed raid.

Now if you want absolutely to experience the thrill of motion, get on a superbike. Laverda, Ducati, Yamaha: their acceleration is literally incredible. They're the only road machines in which I don't have the nerve to go to maximum revs in any gear.

Indeed, they get close to my definition of a 'supercar', which is an ever more elusive term, just as 'sports car' once was. My own favourite was the Porsche 550A. It was so bike-like in its proximity to other traffic on British roads and as sensitive and responsive as a Stradivarius violin.

All of the nineteen cars in *Story of the Supercar* have been tested by people who know what they are talking about and are not afraid to 'push the envelope'. But the one unmentionable factor is price, or rather cost. A 250GTO is gorgeous, but how about half a mile of salmon river (both banks) and 15,000 acres of hill in Scotland for the money? Or a lovely white Kensington town house with a garden and a lot of wisteria? Or, if you prefer living in hotels, £2000 cash every week from the money market?

This is the great dilemma of all collecting – how do you trade off the pleasures of ownership, the enhancement of your quality of life, and hard reality? If it's fun and thrills and enjoyment of machinery that you like, and you've a big barn, let me suggest a portfolio – an old Mercury Allard, a VW Beetle, an Impala convertible, a decrepit 2CV, a Willys Jeep and a 1943 Dodge Command Car. That will give you all of these things, plus a stack of dollar bills, in exchange for the least valuable vehicle listed in *Supercar*.

And don't forget, fashions change. Look at the chapter 'Death in the Afternoon'. I won't spoil the book by revealing what it shows . . .

Today's ultimate supercar might actually be a helicopter

Alan also wrote some columns for Classic Cars' *sister publication,* Superclassics. *In this issue the magazine featured supercars with the McLaren F1 on the cover. Alan argues against low-slung hyper-performance machines for use on today's motorways. He suggests instead the rather more practical Porsche 911, Audi Quattro, his diesel Land-Rover and Bentley Continental – or a Hughes 500 helicopter.*

What *is* a supercar?

I can remember a time when practically the most contentious question that could be discussed was 'What is a Sports Car?'

Performance, agility and protection had all to be balanced (just as they are in the design of, say, a Main Battle Tank) and opinions were strongly held – often to the extent that an intellectual, sometimes even a moral, opprobrium could be attached to those holding a different opinion.

Fun, and competition-worthiness, used to come top of the list. But then competitiveness (*not* the same thing), slicks, sponsorship logos and the rest made it impossible to commute and compete in the same machine. And soon along came the 'sports saloon'. Remember a thing called the MG YB?

The writing was on the wall. No one had the top down on motorways. Your passenger would be washing her hair for real, and in quite a bad mood, by the time that you reached the hotel. So along came the 911, that wonderful, flicking, slicing, slewing (occasionally) road capsule. Making the transition from 'sports' to 'super' car and claiming for twenty-five years – many would say even to this day – pre-eminence.

It is the perennial conflict between ease of travel (however swift) and *excitement*.

This week I drove from Zermatt to Saltwood in twelve hours in the most efficient (but least 'super'-eligible) vehicle – the Discovery TDi. Before you laugh, consider two things. The tank had to be filled only once, giving a minimum twenty-minute elapsed-time advantage over a Ferrari or Bentley Turbo. And what my wife calls the 'wobble factor' restricts autoroute cruising to 85 mph, a mandatory discipline that saves more time (and money) at gendarme interception points. Excitement, though, nil.

If from my own experience I list, in order of age, cars that I find really exciting, there are in fact remarkably few:

The 1908 chain-drive Locomobile '40' with 11 litre, T-head, Wisconsin engine that ran in the Vanderbilt cup. Most Heroic.

The 1928 26/220 Mercedes that held (and for all I know, still holds) the Cambridge to Oxford record time. Best Looking.

The 1930 Hewitt 8 litre Bentley with outside exhausts and a sump full of Castrol R which (when I owned it) had done fewer than 10,000 miles. Most Authentic.

The 1938 Embiricos 'streamliner' 4¼ litre Bentley. Most Willing.

The 1953 ex-Villoresi Ferrari 340 Mexico. Most Dangerous.

The 1955 Ferrari 750 Monza Scaglietti two-seater. Most Flattering.

The 1966 Lola with Chevrolet 'porcupine' engine. Most Loathsome.

I think in all honesty that, with the exception of the Lola (itself a precursor, with the GT40, of the closed, vibration-tormented, suffocating spaceship school), I would prefer any of these to the McLaren. Although plainly, if ground-covering is the principle criterion, a 'pre-owned' Audi Quattro at, say, £12,000, will get there before the others.

I also have one idiosyncracy. I can't bear sitting low down. A constantly changing view of the differential casings on belching HGVs is something I can do without.

So these days I drive the new Bentley Continental 'S' (built only to special order and with certain enhancements over the

'R', such as a viscous axle and the Zytec engine). Very fast, quiet and strong, without the scuttle shake that mars the Azure, it comes nearer to being a perfect supercar than anything else at the present time. But it is still too heavy. Four hundredweight off (is this now an illegal sentence, by the way?) would allow different spring-rates, and the brakes might last a little longer.

Harder pads would help here, too. But then on a cold morning the hung-over Forex dealer would, at first application, plough straight on into the rush-hour traffic at his home roundabout.

The two oldest moans, which have been around since 1906, are 'Where can you find the roads?' and 'Why do you need so much power?' They are just getting a little bit harder to answer with conviction. So perhaps it's time, literally, to move up. The Hughes 500 costs £580,000, will carry five plus luggage, cruises at 160 mph, and is fun to 'drive' on country roads following the Catseyes but five feet off the ground. Traffic you can hop over at the last minute – itself a challenging calculation. 'Chicken' with a difference.

Look for things the rest won't see and the auction room becomes an exciting place

The electric atmosphere generated at auction really appealed to Alan. As an inveterate gambler he relished the challenge of keeping the auctioneer down to the best price. He knew the rules of engagement; at one auction, as we entered the tent, he spied the auctioneer and walked in the opposite direction of the car we were about to inspect. He explained that he didn't want to be seen looking at this particular Bentley as this would forewarn the auctioneer.

Almost since the classic car movement was in its infancy I have bought and sold at auction. I love them. For some years, before I was a Member of Parliament, I could often make quite a good turn without even leaving the tent. I recall doubling my money (£200) on a Humber staff car, and being mightily relieved to get out of a Lagonda M45 fabric saloon for a profit of £15. When the hammer goes down you can be exultant at victory or, just as often, filled with remorse.

Nowadays I don't have time or the keen knowledge to enter the fray. It's hard to keep up with different influences, cartels, 'rings', 'distress' sales, 'washing' profits, 'dumping' stock, and the rest.

The biggest pressure on price, however, remains fashion. It is barely twenty years since the hottest properties were Duesenbergs and Rolls-Royce Phantom IIs with exotic coachwork. At the time, sports racing cars, even with combat histories, barely came into it.

I recall one Sotheby's sale. In what's called the 'special' car park, a kind of annexe to the main hall, a couple of Dutchmen were literally begging passers-by to give cash for their (slightly dog-eared) 300SL roadster. The 'distress' price had already fallen to £1300. 'Give 'em eight-fifty,' growled a hard-bitten dealer chum (now, alas, with God). I think he ended up as owner for £925.

Fashion is not, of course, the same as taste. Though good taste is a reliable guide to what, over the long term, will be fashionable.

The rise and rise of the Barn Car is a good example – this phenomenon has reached such a point that I've known cases where a car has dropped in value by being washed and having inflated tyres.

Then there is tension between shiny or restored cars and good examples. The two qualities rarely coincide. Careful inspection at the viewing, though, should soon reveal how thorough, or slipshod, a restoration has been.

Look for the usual signs – traces of overspray on door or boot rubbers, wrong combinations of trim and, of course, non-matching numbers. A very shiny new chassis plate on the bulkhead puts me on my guard. On a genuine car, chassis numbers may appear on the inside rim of the bonnet and even the carburettor air-intake cowl.

Whether or not a car will drive well is harder to tell. I look for a grubby engine compartment. If nuts and gaskets have not been disturbed for a long time it probably won't have wooden pistons. Never believe unsubstantiated claims of low mileage.

This is the fun of buying at auction. So much more like poker than arguing with the vendor in a showroom or on the pavement.

But beware the pitfalls. Towards the end of bidding, if the auctioneer is looking to the side of the room he's probably only looking at the radiators. Don't be duped; stop bidding. You should get the car for less afterwards. Never, incidentally, fall for the 'just a smidgen more' ploy in after-sales negotiations. The vendor will be in a complete panic and hugely relieved just to settle below the reserve.

Every sale has its flavour. Discovering who will be on top, the auctioneer or the punter, is fun. There will be electricity in the air, too. All compounded by rivalry, acquisitive intent and a certainty that – at the end of the day – a lot of cash is going to change hands.

Alan has a pop at one of Britain's favourite marques and suggests that classic car prices need a shake-out

This is another piece that Alan wrote for Superclassics *magazine. He indicates a preference for big, fast and practical cars over supercars and then goes on bravely to predict the prices for cars at an impending auction. He was largely correct in his predictions.*

It is a well-known law of journalism that editors like their contributors to be 'controversial'. This generates indignation, which leads to correspondence, and gets the paper talked about. And has never been any problem for me. But I do know that if one expresses an opinion – particularly if it is critical – about a car, you only offend the people who own, or admire, one. Start talking about prices, though (or rather *values*: not always the same thing), and practically everyone gets cross. So here goes.

Today the market is more or less seized solid. Dealers are out of credit and won't buy for stock. Vendors think prices are 'too low'. Buyers are waiting for them to drop further. In the end what drives the market is not what a car is 'worth', but whether you want one. And how many others, at the time, also want one.

Three of the cars starring in this particular issue illustrate very well the cross-permutation of value and (real or notional) desirability. The Lamborghini Miura epitomizes the Italian sports exotic. Wonderful fun on your own circuit, but designer-noisy, vicious to drive and won't start on a wet day. At its weakest, like Ferraris, when A and B are a long distance apart. I well recall, in the summer of 1968, leaving Turin in a Mercedes 600 full of children, au pair, spades and flippers and getting to Capri a complete ferry-sailing ahead of a friend in a Miura who had started at the same time. The Miura was the same price when new at £7000, peaked at £145,000, is now £45,000 – yet still a good way ahead of the 600 as a store of value.

Pre-war Lagondas, like 'WO' Bentleys, are in the blue chip category, and their prices are less distorted by investment hoarding and forced sales. But even the gilt-edged can fluctuate through a 10 per cent price band over a year. Timing is critical.

As for Aston Martins, they are probably still the most overvalued classic cars. Their reputation rests largely on snobbery – a direct line running from a bemonocled Laurence Pomeroy in the early 1950s, through David Brown, who maintained a racing team to compensate for the fact that he was five feet and one quarter inches high, and only won at Le Mans after Jaguar and Mercedes stopped entering, to James Bond and the poor Prince of Wales stranded by an 'electrical fault' on the Hammersmith flyover at rush hour.

Nonetheless, snob appeal is a real contributor to value, otherwise you wouldn't get people paying £275 (or is it £2750?) for a T-shirt made in Taiwan simply because it has a small green crocodile embroidered over the left breast. So there will be no special penalty for the Aston in my suggested new price structure. Which goes like this:

Since the great peaks, most prices have come back by two thirds. It's not enough. Halve them again and you might finally induce the shake-out which, Wall Street analysts teach us, is necessary before a market regains liquidity following a slump.

An example from my own experience: in November 1981 I was shown the most original C-type (chassis XKC 013) I have ever set eyes on. Tiny mileage, nothing disturbed, engine never opened. Three weeks later it sold for £985,000. Cash, produced by some crazy merchant bank, advised, I assume, by a Leeson clone that it was good security for a 100 per cent loan. Two years later I bought it from the deceased owner's estate for £310,000. What's it worth today? That's right, half. £155,000.

Because worth can only mean: what is the sum for which a purchaser will actually write out a cheque? No part-exchange, or SOR, or POA. Cash. Now, ahead of the hammer, and insecure in the knowledge that by the time *Superclassics* is on the news-stands the results will be known to all, I take a look at the

Coys and Brooks catalogues for their end-July [1995] sales. Here is a random list of 'real' values, taken by the simple expedient of halving the low estimate (but including the 15 per cent buyer's premium):

1934 Lagonda M 45 £21,950; 1937 Bentley PW 4¼ £8725; 1959 Kieft Climax sports-racing £5750; 1964 Lancia Flaminia £9200; 1991 Jaguar XKSS (replica) £28,750; 1970 Jaguar Series 2 E-type £10,350; 1985 Ferrari 288GTO £114,250; 1935 Bentley 3½ litre VDP tourer £39,750; 1939 SS100 3½ litre £57,500; 1931 Rolls-Royce PII sedanca (replica) £37,000; 1904 Mercedes Simplex 28 hp tourer £115,000.

This is a game anyone can play, with any catalogue. But even at these levels would you honestly be happy writing out the cheque? If not, this means that the market has not yet stabilized.

Size matters but a huge engine isn't always impressive. Not when it sends you into a hedge

Big, lusty and powerful engines are more restful than high-revving screamers. Alan was right about the Bentley Arnage engine: with the Volkswagen takeover the venerable 6¾ litre engine of the Bentley Arnage Red Label has been suitably cleaned up to meet current emission standards and is back under its bonnet once again. It seems that Bentley drivers like Clark didn't take to the fussy, turbocharged replacement unit that BMW tried to foist on its customers. No, effortless amounts of locomotive shove is a much more civilized way to travel. Incidentally, the most powerful car Alan ever drove was a Lola Can-Am racing car with a 750 bhp Chevrolet Porcupine engine.

Ah. The delight of cubic inches! For a long time the Americans had a saying: 'There's no substitute for . . .' and in the early 1950s this was certainly borne out by results at their own circuits. The beautiful and well-bred XK could only just stay ahead of the Mercury-engined J2 Allard. And once a 5.4 litre Cadillac was shoe-horned into the chassis there was really no point in tearing the XK to pieces in pursuit. You lost.

Practically every car made has been improved by fitting a larger engine. Even the 'WO' Bentleys were transformed from Fordson tractor (the 3 litre) to quite reasonable Massey Fergusson 6-90 (the 4½) after increasing engine displacement by 50 per cent. And who now wants to buy a Jaguar 2.4? No one. But the Mark II 3.8 – provided you can find one that isn't suddenly going to break in half – is, I still maintain, the four-door classic of all time. While today the VW Golf, a very good car, has been transformed by the insertion of a V6 into a formidable performer on the road.

Similarly, I'm sceptical of cars that on the back of improved technology claim the same or equivalent performance but have had their engine size reduced. We all know what happens: a couple of old women in the boardroom sign up to the goody-goody 'Speed Kills' doctrine, arguing it's greener and therefore better for the corporate image; the sales team counter that they can't offer customers new models that are unable to out-accelerate the old ones; then the poor boffins are sent off to extract the same amount of power from a smaller block.

This they do with the usual textbook devices: altered valve timing, higher compression, more sensitive engine control – all, of course, at higher rpm. Theoretically the power output may be the same, but the car feels different. The new Bentley Arnage, where the design team had to induce the same output from 4.6 litres as formerly came from 6.7, is a lovely drive. But they had to resort to two-stage supercharging, and gone is that restful feeling of effortless domination of other traffic you find in the Continental 'R'.

A very big, effortless engine will always give a memorable drive but what about the steering? Huge engines often make cars nose-heavy. Caught unawares on a tightening radius you may find yourself 'ploughing'. I don't at all like having to set the car up for a corner – at any speed. I hate using my expensive tyres to drift and scrub. My definition of agility is cornering (and changing direction) 'on rails'.

It is impossible to find a car, even today, that will really do this. The first Golf GTI used to but then it, *in extremis*, would transmute into four-wheel drift. I suppose the 911 comes closer than anything else – but don't ever take it for granted, especially if there are leaves on the line.

The Citroën 'Light Fifteens' of 1938–40 did it better than anything else I know. And they made very few three-seater roadsters with a dicky at the back. What a wonderful thing that would be to find pristine – perhaps in some dry, high-roofed barn in the Auvergne?

But until the vehicle is made that goes immediately where you point it, and which at the same time accelerates – significantly – in harmony with your right foot pressing to the floor, the ultimate classic will continue to elude us.

Bring out your dead. Soon there will be a time when the breaker's man will come calling for the corpse of your dead 1990s classic

Modern or future classics are difficult enough to predict, but there is another problem with them. Many will simply not last long enough to become appreciated or collectable. Alan refers to the 'thirty-year rule' where current buyers chase the cars that were in when they were teenagers, but the cars that today's teenagers will one day want as classics are too full of electronic gadgetry, which will render most of them inert after their sell-by date. The answer, according to Alan, is to go back in time. Vintage cars are easy to fix and maintain and are the better investment in a static market. They offer a good deal of driving enjoyment, as is evident in the Bulletin of the Vintage Sports Car Club, *where many young drivers are seen in action at race meetings, hill climbs and club meets.*

As I write, a wall of metal is crashing through the auction houses. It's too early to predict, but I get a strong feeling that the forecast I made in this column a couple of years ago is coming true. I said then the market isn't really going to pick up until the price/demand mechanism is allowed to operate. I suggested that if you really want to find the pricing floor, where the greedy seller and suspicious buyer are going to have to meet, then you must take the lowest estimate in the catalogue – and then halve it.

At present really important pieces, with verifiable history, will still fetch high prices – particularly if two rich men are bidding. Or they'll sell privately through a broking dealer. But run-of-the-mill classics, especially if clumsily repainted, are jolly hard to shift.

We are hearing a lot about the 'thirty-year rule'. It argues that the strongest sector will be those cars that today's managerial yuppies pined for in their teens.

Strong? The best piece of kit around in 1968 without any doubt whatsoever was the Mercedes 300 SEL 6.3. It would eat anything, and in comfort, too. But at an auction it's the archetypal bad seller. While even the thirty-year-old E-type seems at present levels more likely to induce tyre-kicking than cheque-writing.

But I've a more fearful premonition. And it's where the thirty-year rule falls down. If we try and fast-forward (buying ahead, the stock market calls it) to anticipate the next trend we encounter a strange phenomenon. Many cars of the 1990s, even the late 1980s, simply won't last the required thirty years. They're too clever. Those brilliant engine management systems go glitchy – and there is nothing you can do, except replace the entire box. This isn't cheap and after a bit – say another twenty years – they will be 'no longer available'. The breaker's yards will fill up with lovely-looking cars that are completely incapable of movement.

So my tip for depressed markets would be this: don't try to anticipate – go even further back in time. The sector used to be called Vintage, but anything with a rigid front axle will do.

All you must do is avoid any car with rubber gloves, grommets or washers around a moving part and be particularly distrustful of 'sealed-for-life' springs and unions. The incredibly durable Rolls-Royce Silver Ghost has seventy-eight separate lubrication points that have to be oiled with a syringe! (Although, admittedly, this was as much to prevent the chauffeur hanging round the pantry harassing parlour maids as any need for maintenance.)

No, don't be intimidated by age and old technology. If a union has got dry all you do is disassemble, buff, relubricate and put it together again. And don't forget that as well as being rewarding to work on this kind of machinery, it can also be exhilarating to drive.

Get hold of a copy of *Bulletin of the Vintage Sports Car Club* and you will find endless pictures of hyper-stark little flyers being hurled around the club hills and circuits. Low on pulling power they may be but they're packed with personality and not extravagant to buy.

Dip into the 'thirty-year' fold if you wish, but Vintage classics are probably as good an investment as any in a stagnant market.

Always buy for love, not money

This is a piece Alan wrote for the **Financial Times** *in January 1997. What he says about the value of E-type Jaguars still stands today, early in a new millennium. He continues to support 'scruffy original' over 'new restoration'. Alan concludes that the best reason for buying an old car is for enjoyment, not profit.*

What are the factors that underpin the classic car market? Separately or in combination, they haven't changed. Nostalgia; male display; toytime and 'investment'.

The good news is that prices have been falling, erratically, for the last two years. So the whole market place should be much looser. But there are today for practically every make, even including real offered-not-bid lines like 25 hp Rolls-Royces and post-1970s Ferraris, what traders on the Forex call 'support levels'.

First, the male jewellery market: chunky beach medallions. Here the punters are mainly for E-types, Ford Thunderbirds of the 1950s and, with diamond inlay, pre-war Mercedes 500s. This sector hasn't been too strong lately. Although why it doesn't start to pick up with all these dealers' bonuses flying around, I don't know. Maybe fashion has moved on. If so – good. Because it must be said that people who genuinely love old cars don't really like them being too valuable. It restricts the fun that can be had; insurers impose mileage limitations; and gawpers say wot's-it-worth-then-guv whenever you're stationary. I myself feel more comfortable with something shabbily original, which is worth less than the cost of 'restoring' (a process that usually means ruining it by depersonalization; clearly no one in the motor trade went to the Christie's sale of the Houghton/Sassoon furniture last winter, where seventeenth-century pieces in darned and battered original silk made double the price of those that had been stylishly reupholstered by some decorator).

If acquisition does not involve significant financial outlay, then it's easier to dabble, and accumulate.

But somewhere, inevitably, the laws of supply and demand cut in. It is still, and will always remain, easy to collect Reliant Robins or Triumph Heralds. But you need to be rich to own more than one Vintage (i.e. made at Cricklewood and designed by W.O.) Bentley. The 3 litre, the archetypal blue-chip classic, was, five years ago, worth £150,000. This summer I bought one that hadn't been started for forty years for less than the price of a new Toyota Supra.

I can honestly say that I don't think it will ever fall in value. But that was not the reason I wrote the cheque. Any concept of investment, even at the back of your mind, will usually end in disappointment. Just as it does in the field of fine art. Look at what happened to the British Rail pension fund, advised by Sotheby's, no less. Not on the basis of what was beautiful or neglected – but what was likely to go up.

Harder to resist is nostalgia. And with it a delicious Walter Mitty substitution of identity. I have a C-type Jaguar, one of the very early series that had drum brakes and won the 1951 Le Mans race – the first British victory for twenty years. And every time I get behind the wheel I can fantasize about being one of the great drivers of that epoch, my schoolboy heroes.

Or you can step straight into fiction – what say you to an 8 litre Bentley saloon: long bonnet, low windscreen; the romance of the Great North Road with leather luggage and gun-cases reeking of saddle soap on the back seat? 'Several times I saw the needle rise past the 100 mark, finally drawing up on the gravel by Hunting Tower to catch the setting of the midnight sun' – as from any John Buchan thriller of the 1920s. This is probably what makes Vintage Bentleys so saleable: they straddle both the nostalgia and the toytime market. But if you just enjoy fiddling with *wholesome* machinery and no nonsense about metric spanners, then Alvis Speed Twenties or even 'Baby' Austins are therapeutic.

I used to do a lot of motoring in a Porsche 911, and certainly no classic will match it for speed and agility. But lately it seems to have been receding further and further back in the Barn. Increasingly I find myself journeying in a 1995 Bentley Continental 'S' (I had an 'R' for two years before that), the best combination, I suppose, of speed and protection; plus a wonderful and instantly responsive ventilation system.

Yet there remain many drives for which I would prefer a classic. My most memorable experience of the decade was the great Alpine Commemorative Rally of 1993, fourteen days and every pass in the Alps, including Slovenia. The only car eligible was the Rolls-Royce Silver Ghost, and not one of the seventy entrants broke down. I would love to take the Ghost back to the Dolomites and do some exploring, but this time not against the clock.

While for a tour of the Loire Valley, or practically any other journey that you could visualize on *routes départementales*, there is still nothing to match the Citroën DS, preferably in Decapotable form. The DS must be the cheapest practical classic still easily available. But before taking the plunge, read carefully that new directory, written by John Reynolds and just published by Bayview Books. And above all remember this rule – buy only because you love the machine; not because you want to show off, or think you will double your money.

The best cars have been to finishing school. They exude charm, balance and obedience

Another rather obscure British classic car, the Jensen 541, is tipped as being a good buy. It's a class act and is still undervalued. Alan is ruminating about classics of the future but comes back to cars simply made of the best materials and beautifully put together, like his Bentley R-type Continental, one of the best cars ever made. Certainly that's at the top end of the market but he does mention, although disparagingly, the Golf GTI and Peugeot 204. A good one (and there are plenty about) will be an affordable option for an impecunious driver wanting a bit of motoring action.

Sometimes we play at spotting the classic of the future, either from among what is currently available in the showroom, or from cars that were around in the past but have somehow been overlooked. It's the intellectual equivalent of prowling an abandoned stately home in search of a barn car. Much the same ploy is practised in the world of fine art by dealers and critics, who, discovering the work of a forgotten artist, try to make him fashionable and thus expensive.

But let us be clear about one thing at the outset. If a car is rare it is usually because very few were made; and if very few were made it is because nobody much wanted to buy one new. The reason being because right from the outset it seemed to be a bit of a turkey. (I exclude, of course, that select little group so exotic and expensive – like the Bugatti Royale or the Ferrari Superamerica – that practically no one could afford them in the first place. Although, come to think of it, both these cars had turkey-like qualities also.)

Thus I would be very careful of secondary classics. If something is ugly, slow and badly assembled (like most British products in the 1950s and 1960s) the fact that there are very few left seems an argument for leaving them well alone. I don't want to upset owners by naming marques, but which would you rather have as a classic runabout – a beaten-up Minor woodie or a low-mileage Hillman Avenger?

When drifting round today's showrooms, it is even harder to make confident predictions – with the sole exception, of course, of the very last two-wheel-drive Porsche 911s. The first Peugeot 204s were lovely, even friskier than the more durable VW GTI, but all made of tin and, bought second-hand, are likely to hide all manner of boy-racer horrors.

How about the amazing *Brabus* Mercedes then? A 7-plus litre V12 shoe-horned into the SL roadster, it guaranteed 208 mph. And *eight*, eh? I'm glad I wasn't in the passenger seat when they clocked that last bit. The Germans are extremely thorough in their engineering, particularly in chassis and suspension response; but exceeding 150 is disagreeable enough even in the highly aerodynamic McLaren – never mind in a roadster configured for cruising along the promenade at Sylt.

No, point-and-squirt design is not enough to make a future classic. True classics have human attributes – charm, balance, durability, obedience. Qualities outside the comprehension of a floor salesman.

We must look to what is the greatest of post-war classics: the Bentley Continental of the 1950s. How many are still around? Under 200, plus eight or nine of the S-type successor that were still fitted with manual gears. Yet it should not be too difficult to follow their example today. No hydraulics; no electric boxes; no climate control; just a set of round gauges that monitor every mechanical function. And a big six-cylinder petrol engine with a very high final drive and a close-ratio gearbox. Everything most carefully machined and assembled.

Probably the nearest anyone has got to it so far is the Jensen 541. And just as the Bentleys lost something (in my view) when they changed the six for a V8, so did the charm of the Jensen start to wane when a Chrysler engine supplanted the original Austin.

Perhaps this is the answer to that most exclusive of all design quests – how to build a classic from scratch. But in the meantime – there's a tip for something trading below its real value.

This classic car addiction is a cash-gobbling octopus

During the 1960s and 1970s, before he became an MP, Alan was deriving a great deal of his income from trading cars. He was trying to pay his overheads and gambling debts by turning over a few old cars. Allegedly, he was once trying to close a sale with a dealer in a London Mews but the price differential of the car he was interested in was too much – about £3,000. Eventually Alan suggested gambling for the difference. The backgammon board was brought out. He lost, which, as the Diaries *record, happened more often than not.*

How much should you spend on a classic? The first one I bought cost £30 (the equivalent of £400 today). The term classic was barely known, still less recognized in those days. I simply fancied something that was different, had stacks of personality and yet entailed a very small outlay.

It was a 3½ litre Bentley with a grotty but elegant 'close-coupled sportsman's' coachwork (coupé for those unfamiliar with 1930s sales jargon). The brakes pulled and the engine felt as if it was giving about 30 bhp. We limped home, anxiously escorted by my wife in an ID Safari full of fidgety children. Not long after, I sold it for £110, having had a lot of fun. It was the start of my infatuation with Derby Bentleys and I now claim to know more about them than anyone else.

This was the beginning of my enthralment with the huge multi-tentacled and insatiable monster that is classic car addiction. Within a year I was a full-blown enthusiast, overdrawing at my bank, opening new accounts and over-drawing at them too. Dealing by 'leveraging' (part-exchanging against other classics, inevitably with additional cash input); ruining my eyes scanning *Exchange & Mart*; and following up the small ads in *Motorsport* at the crack of dawn. I once arrived at an address where a 1936 Hotchkiss drophead had been advertised for £250 to find two dealers actually fighting on the pavement, while the widow peeped nervously out from behind her lace curtains.

My family became uneasy. Some of these hunks of metal wouldn't even belch into life after being towed behind our Land-Rover for half a mile. Phantom IIIs were the worst; they were so heavy they often broke the tow-rope. There seemed no money for anything else. I was in the obsessional condition shared by fellow fanatic Simon Raven, whose telegraphic response to his wife's entreaty, 'Send cash. Self and baby starving' was the laconic injunction, 'Eat baby.'

But this was a period when the market moved up at practically every sale. It was hard to lose money when you parted with something. But tempting, also, to hold on to things in case they went up even further. After some time it became apparent that classic cars are not 'investments' (this is just dealer-speak for 'bound to go up, old boy'). Strictly speaking an 'investment' is a home for money that will yield a regular dividend. Its value improves as the dividend grows. Far from paying a regular dividend, a classic, once acquired, will erode the bank balance. Sometimes it can be like opening a vein.

But there is a substitute for financial yield on a classic. And it's much more important. It's the fun of driving your car or, if you are that kind of person, the therapy you undergo from polishing it.

To the beginner I would give this advice: don't spend capital, or get into debt, with your first purchase. Pay for it out of income. At the start you must be strong-minded. Some cars won't drain you – the 240Z, the Beetle, the Willys Jeeps, the corrugated 2CVs and Mercedes 'taxi' sedans – but others definitely will.

In the evenings educate yourself by plotting high/low-value charts on graph paper. Include every car from a flat-floor E-type to a Minor convertible. With your mind bursting with market savvy, then, and only then, will you be ready to tame the monster of classic addiction.

Infatuated by Derby Bentleys: the full rundown on these underrated cars

This piece on Derby Bentleys must have been written in the late 1960s, judging by the prices Alan quotes. He refers to Rolls-Bentleys, which are now more commonly known as Derbys, or as Silent Sports Cars. They were built by Rolls-Royce at the Derby factory; refined and sophisticated, they are very different to the big and heavy Vintage 'WO' Bentleys.

This is a knowledgeable and detailed account written by someone who understands their discreet charm.

In spite of resolute whistling-past-the-graveyard by influential figures in the clubs and in print, the prices of Vintage★ machinery have remained obstinately high on a plateau attained some three to four years ago after a meteoric ascent. The reasons for this have been widely discussed; probably the most convincing is the steadily diffused aura of 'status' and capital gain with which Vintage ownership has become endowed. Any qualified psychologist will tell you that, after the sexual urge, these are the two most powerful motivating forces in Western society. (And there is a strong sexual element, too, in an 8 litre bonnet, but we'll leave that for another time!)

This price rise has had some beneficial effects. It has ensured that the majority of Vintage cars, being now extremely valuable, are correspondingly well cared for; and it has infused fresh vigour into the clubs which, once seen as isolated bodies of eccentrics, now find themselves regarded as the priesthood of a new, with-it cult. But it has had one unfortunate result, in that Vintage

★ I use the term 'Vintage' in the lay sense, being anything eligible for VSCC events.

ownership is virtually excluded on economic grounds until one reaches middle age.

It is not only the first cost, but the fact (or heresy) that these days it is no longer practicable to consider exclusively Vintage motoring. It may be all right for an eccentric bachelor in Wilts, but is it really acceptable under current conditions of traffic density and annual mileage, for *one*? One's wife needs a runabout; one's children, dog(s), carry-cot, 'Bucky Gate', underwater flippers, etc., etc., require a station wagon; and oneself likes something reasonably taut and agile for getting around. Consequently a good deal of money, as well as space, is a prerequisite of Vintage ownership. (Incidentally, this matter of space is absolutely fundamental, and I strongly caution those who do not have it to read no further. Any attempt to cherish a Vintage car under a tarpaulin always ends in tears.)

However, there is a gleam of hope in this price inflation factor: namely, that there is a strong element of fashion in it. And, as in the art market or the Stock Exchange, the way to protect one's investment is to forget about fashion and go for quality. Certain cars – the Silver Ghost, the SS100 – are highly fashionable, and one can see why. Others, such as the Bull-Nose Morris, are inflated for less obvious reasons. Still others seem to have been left out altogether, and of these the most outstanding example (and one that is bound to get caught up soon) is the Derby or Rolls-Bentley, which can still be bought in running condition for as little as £150.

The advantages of the Rolls-Bentley may be summarized thus:

(1) It is not so slow as to make long journeys painful.
(2) It is extremely durable.
(3) The majority of parts are still available new from the makers...
(4) ...and a sufficiently large number were made for there to be at any given time a good float of second-hand parts.
(5) It is pleasant to work on.
(6) People don't laugh when you go by.

These are all incontestable virtues (unless you like being laughed at) and to them are added qualities that are less definable but which every Vintage enthusiast will recognize: the thrill of driving a long bonnet and P100s into the night or across the Downs on a summer's morning; the extreme precision and solidity of the secondary controls; the evocations of an epoch now remote and nostalgic.

Of course, like most Vintage cars passing through a 'cheap' phase, the majority of Derby Bentleys on the market are some-what down in the mouth – at least in appearance. But take heart; a little patience and discrimination can still unearth what is, at the present price levels, a really desirable piece.

First, background reading. There is an excellent profile on this car, and also a paperback digest of contemporary road-tests and articles – *Bentley in the Thirties* – available from Autobooks. You should also study the relevant passages in the definitive Bird & Hallows. Having absorbed all this information you can sally into the market.

There is a very wide differential of something like 12:1 between top and bottom prices. In the past twelve months £2500 has been paid at auction for a Barker two-door saloon with a genuine mileage of 27,000 and also (by repute) for a Vanden Plas tourer with an excellent racing history in recent club handicaps. Both these cars were 3½ litres, but there are several 4¼s featuring regularly in concours that would probably match these figures if they came on the market. I propose, however, to confine my guidance to the price range of £150–£600 – itself a differential of 4:1 and offering ample opportunity for the intelligent buyer to 'beat the market'.

Generally speaking, you can either go for condition or for attractiveness of coachwork – in its widest sense – and to get both together at a reasonable figure would be a stroke of luck. For example, dropheads are invariably worth the same as double saloons of equivalent mechanical condition; modern-looking saloons tend to fetch less than the more vintage styles with trouser-crease wings and exposed front brakes; the lighter alu-minium bodies are nearly always preferable to steel ones.

In this connection, it is worth remembering that Rolls-Royce originally stipulated that no body to be fitted on the new Bentley (in 1934) was to weigh more than 6½ cwt. But only three

And here we have Mr Toad at speed. Alan driving one of his favourite cars – his 1920 Rolls-Royce Silver Ghost – on the 1993 Rolls-Royce Enthusiasts' Club Alpine commemorative run. This was the event where a fellow competitor remarked, 'if he can't afford to maintain his car properly he shouldn't be allowed on the event'. This amused Alan, particularly as his stripped-down Ghost proved to be one of the fastest on the run.

Returning from the Alpine, Alan awaits the Hovercraft back to Saltwood. The event winners, Ian Fraser and Colin Crabbe, are pictured on the left. Alan took a bit of a chance when entering, he did not have time to change the rather old tyres or the oil! Nevertheless the Ghost performed admirably.

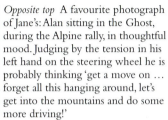

Opposite top A favourite photograph of Jane's: Alan sitting in the Ghost, during the Alpine rally, in thoughtful mood. Judging by the tension in his left hand on the steering wheel he is probably thinking 'get a move on … forget all this hanging around, let's get into the mountains and do some more driving!'

Opposite bottom This was how the Silver Ghost was bought, a basic stripped-down chassis. Here it is photographed in 'barn find' storage, providing a good perch for the Saltwood peacocks before being rebuilt. The Ghost was once the property of Lord Curzon, Viceroy of India, with a Barker limousine body. Alan and son James had the idea of turning it into a fast reconnaissance car, the sort of machine Lawrence of Arabia would have appreciated. The bodywork was kept to an absolute minimum, leaving the car light, fast and in effective Alpine trim.

Above The Rolls-Royce Silver Ghost's Bat mascot in close-up. To appeal, 'a mascot must have been on a car. It must have lanced through driving rain and sleet on the Route Napoleon; stood patiently in the baking sun of the Riviera, strained to vanquish some rival emblem in long and perilous dices down some poplar-lined roads.' Amen!

Left Alan was an enthusiastic mascot aficionado and a number of his cars have unique ornaments at the end of their bonnets. Here he's toasting the Bat on the Ghost after it has successfully completed the 1993 Alpine Commemorative rally.

Above Another firm favourite, a 1953 Bentley Continental originally sold by Jack Barclay Ltd, then bought by Alan in the late Eighties. He could not resist tinkering with the car and replaced the original Flying B on the radiator with his stag's head mascot. He fitted the lighter seats taken from his earlier Continental special, also removed the middle section of the front bumper and painted the number plate directly onto the body below the radiator.

Below This was the first of Alan's new Bentley Continentals, a Continental R finished in a subtle shade of Queen Mother claret. He later replaced this car with a more highly tuned Continental S which had the West of England cloth upholstery and stove-enamelled black wheels for that low-key, hot-rod look.

Above A very rare 1958 Bentley Continental S1, this was the last car to leave Crewe with a manual gearbox. With power steering and a very long back-axle ratio it is a consummate high-speed cruiser. Alan and Jane drove it to Le Mans once and were stopped by the French police because the car does not have seatbelts fitted. 'I think they just wanted to have a good look at the car,' says Jane.

Below As patron of the XK Club Alan hosted a Jaguar meeting at Saltwood in July 1999. Pictured are his lovely XK140 coupé the C-type and the XK 120. Alan was already ill by then and did not have much strength, but Jane recalls how he really enjoyed this Jaguar day, held in glorious weather with the Saltwood gardens in full bloom.

Above A photograph taken just to annoy the purists! A combined weight of over 200lbs of prime Rottweiler on top of the thin aluminium bodywork of the C-type Jaguar. This is a very original car and, although similar to the Le Mans winners, had never been raced much and is therefore largely undamaged and straight. The dogs, Hanna on the left and Leni on the right, did not annoy Alan in the slightest when they jumped onto his £500,000 Jaguar.

Below The C-type being comprehensively climbed upon by much of the Clark family. From the left; Angus, James, Archie, Andrew and Albert. It seems the grandsons have inherited their grandfather's passion for exciting cars.

Above This time the Rottweilers are in the rear of the Scots Grey Bentley with Jane. Unusually for Alan, this car had been restored and, once James had got the wiring and fuel supply sorted out, it ran fine, but they always felt it was a bit of a lorry and not much fun to drive.

Below Another favourite, the now rather bedraggled-looking 1956 Volkswagen. Alan loved this scruffy old 'school-run' Beetle, which he turned into a Q-car by installing the engine from his rusted-out Porsche 356. He added the beautiful Porsche finned aluminium brakes, steering wheel and rev counter and he gamely insisted 'the key modification is to have the Michelin X tyres inflated to 28lbs at the rear and normal crossplies at 26lbs on the front … under some circs the Beetle will actually handle better than the 356'.

Spring 1999, Alan and 'the girls' in Big Red. The large exhaust indicates this is the tuned Bentley Continental 'S', producing around 400bhp. He enjoyed the Continental's 'dominant' power to the full, getting it sideways onto the motorway sliproad or frightening sports-car drivers and anyone else ready to have a go. Alan Clark was a motoring enthusiast from a bygone era. He enjoyed a kaleidoscope of motor cars and owned some of the grandest and most valuable ever built. He could not abide 'rivet counters', or polishers obsessing over a perfect paint job or chassis number. What he enjoyed most was having a dice with someone in a flash sports car and beating him in one of his scruffy old machines. 'Buy what you like, not what you think you should have,' was the encouraging motto from a man who could have owned almost anything in the motoring world.

coachbuilders managed to achieve this: Vanden Plas was the tourer; Mann Egerton with a 'lightweight' four-door saloon and Park Ward with a two-door. The limit was very soon dropped and thereafter, as in the case with every good car since the beginning of time, weights went up, performance went down and engine capacity and output had to be increased.

The following table, culled from contemporary road-tests, illustrates this:

car type	weight in cwt	standing ¼ secs	max speed (best)
3½ litre			
1934 Vanden Plas tourer	29¼	19.2	91
1934 Park Ward saloon	30½	–	92
1935 Park Ward drophead	32½	20.8	90
4¼ litre			
1936 Park Ward saloon	33½	19.4	94
1939 Park Ward saloon	35	–	93
1939 Park Ward drophead	35¼	20.2	88

The Park Ward saloon was an elegant creature in its early days with a stylish sawn-off tail, but it gradually increased in bulk and weight so that the 1937–9 examples are probably the least valuable of all the pre-war Bentleys today. Yet paradoxically the 1936s, the very first 4¼s, were the fastest cars that Bentley Motors built before the war – and anyone who doubts their performance should read Raymond Mays' account of his tremendous drives in one between the various Continental race circuits before the war, and of his setting up a record, on unmade roads, between Cape Town and East London (printed in *Autocar* in November 1944). A 1936 4¼ in original condition would be nice.

While on the subject of performance, it is probably true to say that the evolution of engine output and suspension design has now progressed to a point where the Derby Bentley stands in the same relation to the modern car as the Vintage Bentley did to the cars of the 1940s and early 1950s. This fact is somewhat obscured because good Vintage Bentleys at present greatly out-number good Derby ones (for reasons enlarged on at the beginning of this article) and the beautifully cared-for 3/4½ litre 'WO' car will – *may* – outperform a raddled Derby specimen which hasn't had a spanner on it for 50,000 miles.

But car for car, the 3½ litre will run away and hide from most of the 'WO' models – anyone doubting this could turn to the issue of *Autocar* for 30 March 1934, which ran a comparative test with a 3 litre Speed model; the 3½ litre did 0–60 in thirteen seconds; the 3 litre took twenty-three. In addition, a good Derby car is susceptible to some mild Stage I tuning of a do-it-yourself kind; the three easiest steps are: (1) taking it up to 60,000 from the head; (2) substituting a single straight-through expansion chamber for the existing exhaust system (which is probably rotten anyhow); and (3) removing the fan and fitting an electric unit (Wood-Jefferies is the best). There are further stages of tuning, but before embarking on this, it is safer to be sure of the bottom end's soundness by fitting a full-flow oil filter.

First, though, one must find as good a specimen as possible. In the late 1950s Rolls-Bentleys were worth very little and went through that phase (which nearly every Vintage machine has been through at some stage in its life) of being 'driven into the ground', i.e. where the cost of servicing – much less of repairing or replacing defective components – was equivalent to, or exceeded, the value of the whole car. So why not go on until the thing literally dropped dead? They took an awful lot of killing, but during this period many suffered internal damage so extensive that only a full strip and overhaul would put it right. There are few dealers who will put their money into an 'invisible' improvement of this kind (SAE 60 oil and a restricted duration demo run is a cheaper solution), so the only hope is that it should have been done either by the original owner as part of the car's maintenance, or by another enthusiast who was fond of it.

When you examine one of these cars the vendor will nearly always produce bills. Scrutinize them carefully. Invoices from Bentleys for parts (quoting the car's chassis number) are worth three times as much as a long job-card at Oliver Bash Ltd. Ideally, one is looking for a car with *documentary* evidence (preferably the logbook), showing it to have led a sheltered life. It is worth remembering that, up to about 1952, Rolls-Bentleys would fetch over four figures and were correspondingly well looked after.

You will have to form your own assessment of the car's history, which may range from peaceful storage in the heated garage of a country house to a hectic turnover of owners with suspiciously student-like addresses.

Having examined the documents, next make the static inspection. Coachwork first; open and shut all the doors, windows, bonnet, boot, *observing*. Look for overspray, cracking, rust, aluminium oxidization lifting the paint (unimportant, but convenient for knocking down the price). Put all your weight on the front wings where the sidelight is mounted and press down suddenly. If the car rocks on its springs solidly as one piece, that's a good sign. Try the sliding roof, and inspect the channels and corners. (In fact most cars now have their sliding roofs sealed over, but rehabilitating them is one of the pleasanter and least arduous phases of the restoration.)

The condition of the internal chrome and woodwork are always a good indicator of the way in which the car has been cherished. Naturally the veneers lift and chafe away at the corners and along the top sills, but original veneers are nearly always preferable to a quick re-stain and plastic finish. Some of the very early 3½ litres had solid mahogany or cedarwood fillets, which can be sanded off pale in your workshop and look extremely smart.

Now occupy the driver's seat. Some indicator of the car's total mileage can be drawn from the quality of definition in the lettering on the steering column boss. The enamel starts to go at 60,000 and has virtually disappeared at 100,000, leaving only the cuts of the engraving. If the lettering has gone, let your hand drop to the handbrake and grasp it around the shaft as near to the gate as possible. Then lift upwards. At over 100,000 miles, some vertical play becomes apparent and this increases with mileage. (This is not an infallible test, of course, as the gearbox may have been rebuilt during the car's affluent period.)

Now start the engine. It should fire at once. If it doesn't, it may mean that all is not well in the cylinder head – a sticking valve, a broken piston ring. If it's simply bad tuning, carburettors or ignition out of adjustment – well, that's a sign of poor maintenance. (Here it's worth mentioning that a car need not be rejected out-of-hand because the engine is dead, if it appeals otherwise. But make sure it will turn over on the handle, and that the cylinder head is not cracked. A second-hand cylinder head costs upwards of £45, and they are getting harder to find. Water in the sump sometimes shows itself by the oil indicator needle lying right up against the stop.)

On the assumption that you get the engine running, set the hand throttle to 1,100 rpm and jack up the front of the car. (The vendor is most probably getting the sulks by now.) Look at the brake cable and adjusters and the junction points of the one-shot lubrication system. Dryness and caked dirt are ominous here. Next remove one of the front wheels. They should slide off a treat, but seldom do. Old yellow grease caked hard on the hub splines is a sign of neglect.

All this time you will have been listening to the engine. Tapping and clicking doesn't matter, but if it knocks, or rattles on a trailing throttle, better leave it (unless he'll take less than £100). Switch off, and look at the water-pump greaser; it should be finger tight and, when extracted, found to be full of the correct grade of Castrol grease. While the bonnet is open on the induction side (which of course it will be at this moment), inspect the unions from fuel pump to carburettors via filter casing, all control rods, and the block itself for cleanliness, seepage, etc.

Now comes the moment for the road test. There may be difficulties. Quite likely it will emerge that the car isn't licensed, hasn't got an MOT, or the insurance position is obscure. The probability of the vendor allowing you to drive it is almost nil and in fact there is little you could discover that vigilance during the earlier stages would not have told you already. But the road test can be of help in sealing the transaction. Most of this article is slanted against the vendor, but it is only fair to him to get the haggling over at this stage and agree a figure – subject to nothing dreadful happening on test. Then, if the back axle clunks horribly but the car still appeals, you could try to cut the earlier figure a bit lower.

I may say that you won't get this kind of service from a dealer, as the whole business is going to take at least a couple of hours, and even allowing for the fact that he will have a 75 per cent mark-up on the car, he won't like putting himself out to this extent on a £450 deal. In fact I'm assuming that the readers of *Motor Sport* have enough enthusiasm and savoir faire to shop around. The object is to try to find something that costs less than £400 but which a dealer could wax and vacuum and ask £675 for. On the other hand it must be said that some of the dealers are extremely tolerant and enthusiastic and if you have a part-exchange problem, then it is to them that you will have to go, unless you are extremely lucky, for that is what their big margin is there to take care of.

Below is a table as a very rough guide to safe prices. This is a thankless task, owing to all the variables, but equally one must have *some* guideline. (I am against cageyness on figures, believing that every article offered for sale should be clearly marked with the price — just as every published photo of a woman under thirty-five should state her exact age.)

car type	non-runner	poor	fair	mint
4¼ litre Park Ward saloons, post-1936 (add 10 per cent for MR and MX chassis)	£90	£135	£240	£600
3½ litre coachbuilt saloons	£110	£175	£325	£750
Two-door saloons, fancy closed coachwork on either chassis	[add approx. 25 per cent]			
Dropheads; some sedancas of particular elegance	£250	£400	£575	£1000

Assuming you've clinched a private deal, and fixed the insurance, take the car to the nearest garage and change the oil. This is *mandatory* unless you live under five miles away; that oil could have been in the sump since 1954.

The journey home will be characterized by extremely *slow* driving. In his classic work, the Continental correspondent somewhere expresses the hope that none of his readers will ever be driving at less than 'six-tenths'. Well, on this journey they will. Your chances of driving the car hard and enjoyably in the future may be at stake. Just listen to everything that is happening and watch the instruments.

A high engine-coolant temperature may simply be a weak thermostat shutter spring, or the shutters themselves may be in need of lubrication. There is provision for overriding the thermostat and locking them fully open (a normal engine will then run very cool, but can be blanked off with a piece of aluminium plate according to the seasons). If the oil pressure falls away to below 10 lb, stop, and look at the level. A 4¼ litre will habitually use more oil than a 3½ but don't assume the worst; it may be a simple leak. If the engine stops, the most likely cause will be a block in the fuel system from gummy deposits working free – but no matter; you are shortly going to deal with all this in a systematic fashion. In all cases of engine or other failure, first check the fuses, which are beautifully laid out and labelled in a box on the nearside of the engine bulkhead. You are going to rewire this car sooner or later; if the fuses are popping already, make it sooner.

Once the car is safely in your garage, a Stage I restoration can commence. Far the best beginning is to follow, scrupulously, the directions in the RR Service Pamphlet on 'Recommissioning cars after long periods of storage' – even though 'a long period of storage' is probably the last thing the car has been enjoying. The procedures laid down are hard work, but rewarding, and get one familiar with every part of the car. I strongly recommend against premature dismantling of suspect components. One loses heart (and pieces) and finds reassembly difficult. Besides, you ought to keep the car on the road, to live with it and appreciate its foibles.

It is a good idea to alternate spells on the engine and chassis with attacks on the coachwork. First, thoroughly brush and vacuum the interior; and cut and wax the cellulose (*however* shabby and patchy it may first appear). This improves everyone's morale, especially that of your wife/girlfriend. Then clean all the chrome, starting with the interior. The best substance for this is Autosolvol, at 4/6d per tube. On the exterior chrome you can use this substance with 000 steel wool, and be amazed. New carpets are easily made from the old templates; about four and a half yards will do the trick, although professional trimmers claim to need fifteen. Slightly more skilled, though perfectly feasible, is the fitting of a new head-lining.

As for the leather, you can use Handy Andy – *once* – thereafter repeated applications of Connolly's Hide Food works wonders. At the same time it is a good idea to remove the trim panels, blow out the rust and dust, reopen the drain holes, and check and lubricate the window winding mechanism. These are enjoyable – and not at all costly – tasks, which will transform the interior.

To itemize every stage would carry us on and out the other side of the classified advertisements. But two final recommendations should be made to increase your enjoyment. Buy, read and digest Wheatley & Morgan's *Restoration of Vintage Motor Cars*, every word therein is golden; and in due course, if you're in the mood, join the Bentley Drivers' Club. Some of the 'WO' owners are a bit high-hat about the Derby cars, but this is certainly not true of the secretariat, who are extremely helpful. The club is very active socially, and chats with other owners can save hours of experimentation on your own car.

Total production of Derby Bentleys was 1200 3½ litres, and 1250 4¼ litres. Of these, how many survive?

According to the Registers, there are 61 3½ litres and 119 4¼s in America; 145 and 136 respectively in Britain. Even allowing a 'float' of a further 40 per cent the total is still less than 700 cars, compared with at least 1000 *Vintage* Bentleys. Derby cars are still being broken for spares, but those that survive are being steadily improved in condition as their value rises. Sir Henry Royce took a personal interest in the design and development of the Bentley – indeed, it was the last product where this was the case – and the impact of his personality can be traced throughout the chassis.

In view of the contracting supply and expanding demand, as well as the intrinsic charm and quality of the car, I confidently predict that values will rise, in some cases very steeply, over the next five years.

Optimism takes over after the long winter lay-up and additions to the stable are contemplated

Slipping into trader mode, Alan points out how we often make life simple for salesmen with our optimism after the winter recess. He also advises that the values of some cars are difficult to pin down, so be careful of those offered POA.

Spring is here and the classic car virus, dormant over the winter, comes to life. Its symptom, repressed during the period of fog, drizzle and salt on the roads, is optimism. For the first time in months, fine weather brings cheer to owners and enables their steeds to stand outdoors. It's also kinder to the electrics. Batteries will hold a charge and distributor points haven't closed up tight of their own accord.

So perhaps now's the time to make a cautious addition to the stable? Or set up a useful part-exchange deal? We trawl the showrooms, scan the classifieds. Guidelines that should govern inspection and tyre-kicking are recklessly ignored. Won't start? No problem. The engine looks all right (i.e., the crankcase hasn't actually got a hole in it). That's not rust, it's 'oxidization'. Hood torn, rear window broken? Never mind, 'I always drive with the top down.' Subliminally, we do the salesman's job for him.

I remember being in the mood once, determined to buy a Maserati. The car was in Queen's Gate Place mews, just imported by our greatest dealer-connoisseur, Dan Marguilies. It had not been polished for twenty years and the leather was torn. It had a significant competition history.

But that Maserati absolutely refused to start. It had every-thing – compression, electric spark, fuel in the tank and primed into the carburettor; and Easistart (you know you're in trouble once you resort to Easistart) sprayed into the supercharger. Ah, the supercharger! In there, as in every supercharger I have found on any car, there dwelt a nest of long-lived gremlin bacteria of the kind Chinese explorers are always finding when they open up 1000-year-old tombs.

'Look,' my wife said (I had forced her to accompany me and inspect this wonderful prize), 'if Danny and his entire team can't make it belch into life, how do you think you're going to manage once we get it home?' One last wrenching along the length of the Mews, to no avail, and we departed. Last year I saw that car, doing quite well in a classic race at Oulton Park. Sad.

At that stage no one had mentioned a figure. And this is another symptom of spring. It lowers the tone if you talk about prices. Last Sunday I counted in the motoring section of our leading Sunday paper no fewer than 234 cars offered as 'POA'.

Do you know what these infuriating initials stand for? At the risk of again incurring the wrath of Julius Thurgood and most of the other dealers, I will tell you – Pretty well any Offer Accepted. If the salesman is too uneasy to quote you a price except 'On Application' it simply means he wants to size you up first, and see how much he can take you for. He doesn't know what it's worth any more than you do.

This doesn't happen with houses, or clothes, or in super-markets. Why should we only be told the price of a car when we 'apply'? Myself, I never say, 'How much is it?' which amounts to asking him if he will do the favour of selling you the car. I prefer 'How do you value it?' which, whatever the reply, allows you courteously to disagree.

Further on in this issue there's a feature about Bristols. The Bristol 400 was the second nicest car made in Britain after World War Two (behind only the Bentley R-type Continental). It had a beautiful interior, dashboard, instruments and seats; and the doors shut perfectly. Is there an unrestored one anywhere around? Now, that would truly deserve to be 'POA'. Please treat this column as the 'Application'.

Saltwood

Sunday, 11 November 1990

At last I was free. I climbed into the valiant 'Little Silver' and drove exhilaratingly fast. A lot of the time I was running up to 120 mph, and the very last home straight on the M20 at a continuous 140. Average speed for the whole journey from Plymouth Hoe car park to Saltwood Lodge gates, including fuel stops, contraflow, caravans in Langport, roadwork lights, was 77.8 mph. One of the best ever.

Swapping the Porsche 911 Carrera would be a nightmare, so something else must be done without...

When running a fleet of old cars it's always sensible to have one banker, a car that is entirely dependable, and 'preferably one with a tow hook'. Alan's Porsche 911 is the car he used for fun but it also offered entirely reliable everyday transportation. In typically Clark style, the car was always unwashed and looked scruffy. The front wing had been dented but at the suggestion it be put straight, he huffed, 'Never let a spray gun near a car.' The Porsche still has the wrinkle in the wing and it is still on the button, ready to be fired up and driven off to the Clarks' chalet at Zermatt at the first fall of decent snow.

When the editor suggested themes for this month's column, he said: 'Conclude with what you would give up for a classic – just one sentence ...' But this dilemma is so central to the whole movement that I thought I must share with you my broader thinking.

Give up. That implies something you've already got but could do without. Eye, arm, leg, organ? Wife, child, dog? Beer, wine, coffee, tea? Sorry. But tobacco – be my guest. I have never smoked and would gladly trade it for practically any downmarket classic, like the 173,000-mile Ford Cosworth a friend took me in last week. He drove fast, but not well. It still performed and deserved its rating.

This is cheating. No point in offering to give up something you don't want anyway. Let's talk about cars. What everyday transport could you do without if offered a classic? For me, practically anything made in Spain, Korea, Italy, Yugoslavia, Czechoslovakia, Mexico, Iran or, apart from the Land-Rover Defender Tdi, Britain.

Mind you, the substitute classic must itself have everyday qualities. The early 2CVs, especially with left-hand drive, will go through most UK city traffic like a high-speed dentist's drill. They are less good commuting and dreadful in a big accident. The most practical classic in the bargain basement is the VW Beetle. But don't forget Michelin X on the back and cross-ply on the front, or at the first wet roundabout you may find yourself helping the council workmen with their flower beds. Both 2CV and Beetle are reliable, and their engines will start on a wet morning.

Another pleasing way of getting around, underrated in the UK, is the Aussie Holden, especially practical in Ute (pick-up) form. And I will always welcome any of the 1950s stick-shift coupés from the Eisenhower era. Mercury is probably the best, but Chev, Plymouth and spinner Ford are all tough and fun to throw around.

Once we are in the business of arguing the merits of car substitution, questions of taste and loyalty, as well as crude cash value, come into the equation. My own transport is a Carrera 911 Cabriolet, bought new in 1985, which has never once gone wrong. Incontestably a classic, but also everyday transport. Take anything out of the Louis Vuitton paddock at Hurlingham and say: 'Here you are – but give us the Porsche,' and I wouldn't even consider it.

The catch is you can't really enjoy a classic unless you've a bread-and-butter car as well, preferably one with a tow hook. Some swaps are obvious. If I owned a Primera, I'd jump at any offer to swap it for a beaten-up 240Z, although I hate the Z's plastic seats and there would be an instant bill for retrimming. I don't know if it yet has classic status, but the Mercedes 190 sedan with 2.6 engine is one of the best daily tools you can find. In an elderly Shadow or Bentley 'T', the bellboy may salute you, but the journey will be less enjoyable.

The closer I look, the more I think that it has to be something non-motoring. I'd gladly stop going to the gym, but not skiing. Whisky and gin mean nothing to me, but vodka is useful. As for sport, if there's a ball in it somewhere, I couldn't care less.

Classic cars are important to the lifestyle of anyone who enjoys speed, honest machinery, nostalgia and competition. I suppose that all I would give up for them is something I don't want anyway.

The pleasures of collecting a new car from the factory

This is the May 1985 account in his Motor Journal *of Alan's journey to Stuttgart in Germany to collect his new Porsche 911 Carrera Cabriolet. Although difficult to decipher, it gives a fleeting insight into his first impressions of driving the Porsche.*

Collected car [new] from Hähn (arrived on time at Stuttgart airport: on ILS [?] until 200 ft in pouring rain). Helpful salesman took me there, made confirmatory phone calls, spoke excellent English etc. Staff at Hähns were couldn't-care-less (thus proving this attitude is not a British monopoly) until Echart arrived. He patient, competent, unflappable. Was at first disappointed with *very* dark red leather – looked brown in some lights – but got used to it. Taximan led me back through Stuttgart and on to autobahn – rain drenching. Car very pleasing on the road and feels both alive *and* solid. I drove it around 2–3,500 rpm for first 200km, didn't open it up until getting past a Mercedes using everything in 4th gear on straight leading up to Meich. She is a bit *rough* 'going through the gears', not quite that smooth rush of the turbo, but pleasure to drive all round. Handling still Porschlike; that is to say the front goes light quite easily and one has to be *very* sensitive in 'ongoing' corners at 80+ mph. But that's all part of the personality. She certainly seems amazingly economical, virtually no different from the 356. Marched about at Schaffhausen and wasted time. On autoroutes she *devoured* the distance, cruising at least 30 mph faster than everything else in blinding rain. Arrived in Zermatt in (very) failing light.

DS23, accompanied by Jane

5 October 1983 Tasch to Avallon (via Lons-le-Saunier).

Hood down the whole way. Glorious late autumn weather. Car had been serviced (apparently quite conscientiously) at the Citroën agent in Tasch. But immediately seemed somewhat underpowered. I knew at once – the inevitable symptom – distributor points far too tight. Wouldn't do more than 150km on autoroute and poor response and flexibility. Started imperceptibly 'hunting' and I became worried that it would stall in a block and refuse to restart. Lons-le-Saunier (odious) traffic at a standstill, so we detoured through the old town and emerged by a garage where the ideal Frenchman appeared – intelligent, middle-aged, grey moustache, blue overalls and silly check tamoshanter. He agreed with my diagnosis, fiddled with the distributor (enough?) and we went on our way much better.

Post–war French cars were designed with the accent on speed and durability

The famous Gallic temperament and the long routes nationales through the undulating countryside are the reasons that French cars are so beautiful to drive. A French machine of the 1930s, like the 1938 Figoni and Falaschi (known as Phoney and Flashy to the wags) Delahaye as featured in this issue of Classic Cars, *would be a contender for the Clark Cup at a concours. Having a go at the polishers, Alan would add a five-lap race to any concours to determine the overall winner. Cars have to be driven to be enjoyed!*

His mention of Hurlingham is in reference to the prestigious Louis Vuitton Classic, an upmarket classic car concours held at the Hurlingham Club in Fulham. Here the cars and motorcycles are driven around the croquet greens with considerable enthusiasm. A five-lap race would probably be welcomed by the entrants but the Club – and undoubtedly the well-heeled neighbours – would object vociferously.

Ah. The Delahaye 135! Pre-eminent road car of the 1930s, dominant, when in the mood, at Le Mans Twenty-Four Hours, Monthlery, the Coupe des Alpes, and winner of the great Brooklands epic to determine the 'fastest sports car' in 1939; defeating, on that occasion, such multi-million-pound chips (today's values) as the 2.3 Alfa and the type 57 Bugatti.

The Delahaye was the beneficiary of an infallible formula. Put a big, strong engine into a lightweight, unsophisticated chassis and give it an elegant and skimpy body. Take the Railton, for example, with its 4 litre Hudson straight-eight that made it so 'overpowered' (an unpleasant connotation in the view of 1930s hacks, but to my mind a compliment) that it would climb Brooklands test hill in one bound and actually take off at the summit.

The ultimate hill-climb car of the 1940s and 1950s, the Steyr-Allard, was driven by an air-cooled motor originally conceived to drive a *Wehrmacht* armoured personnel-carrier across the Russian steppe. I saw it put up some incredible times at Prescott and Shelsey. Where is it now? It could have been transformed into a fantastic two-seater that would have made the J2X look like a go-kart.

There is no doubt that the post-war French cars were really terrific. Put any of them on the rostrum today, and the final figure would draw audience applause. The Delage D8-120, the Talbot Darracq, the Delahaye itself and even such relatively mundane remnants as the Onze Légère or the unbreakably tough Peugeot 203. Much of the cachet was attached to the exotic coachwork with which the Grandes Marques were fitted. Letourneur & Marchand, Figoni & Falaschi, Chapron, these names always enhance value.

Their real attraction, for me at least, is how beautifully they drive. I remember asking a respected authority (by coincidence, someone who had bought the 135 demonstrator new in 1936 and kept it for ten years) why this was, and thinking that the answer would relate in some way to their competition pedigree.

Not at all. 'They have to be good,' he told me, 'in order to stand up to French driving.' It was their home environment – dead-straight *routes nationales*, *nids des poules* (potholes), slippery pavé and bad camber – that bred strong engines, springs and shock absorbers and responsive handling. Also that France is the home of one of motoring's most violent phenomena, road rage.

What French drivers have never liked is being unable to get past the car in front. Anyone who ever tries to get round the *périphérique* (the bypass carrying traffic past the centre of Paris) can testify to this. He (or she) who is overtaken (*doublé*) takes it as a personal insult. If they suffer either humiliation, they blame the car. Hence, French cars were built to be fast and durable.

In most cases, they are ideal contenders for the Clark Cup at any posh concours, awarded among the first five cars selected by the judges, with just one catch: the order is determined by the result of an immediate five-lap race – with the entrant at the wheel. I would guess that the strongest entry would usually be a BMW 328, although both the Delahaye and the Darracq would take a lot of beating. One consequence might be that the venue would have to be changed – from Hurlingham to Donington, or Silverstone.

Saltwood

Sunday, 28 June 1987

We had planned our first outside lunch, M. Goisot [from whom the Clarks bought their house wine] and a huge Brie, but forsook it to tend to a baby jackdaw who had got sump oil on his wings and (how, for God's sake?) torn off one of his legs below the knee joint. I thought he was a goner – how *could* he survive? But he had so much fight in him, and his lovely pale blue eyes were so lively that we had to try. Jane washed his wings and tail feathers, rinsing and re-rinsing the Fairy Liquid. He didn't seem to mind; positively enjoyed the warm whirrings of a hair-dryer. We stuffed a couple of worms down his throat and left him to gain strength in a basket with a heat bulb glowing over. In no time he appeared to make a full recovery and later that evening, after being returned to the wild, actually *flew* from the sleeper pile to the yew tree by the long garage. Cheered by this, I started the Silver Ghost and went for a drive.

On a fine evening there are very few pleasures comparable to driving a light, open Ghost on country roads. Some will get it from waiting for salmon to take, in dark peat pools, but I am too impatient, and can't stand the midges. In a Ghost you waft along, high enough to look over people's hedges, noiseless enough (as was the original intention) to leave horses unscared. It started at once, of course, although I hadn't been near it since last November. No (*no*) modern car would have done this. Because the Rolls-Royce Silver Ghost has – except for the magneto which sparks on a turn – not one single piece of electrical equipment. No battery (flat) or pumps (stuck) or solenoid (up the creek, Squire) or 'black box' (I'm afraid we're talking about a factory replacement unit, sir, at £873 plus VAT). There are twenty-one separate actions, all of them involving beautifully crafted mechanical linkages, from turning on the gravity petrol feed to actually cranking the starting handle. And after they have been completed in the correct sequence it will – infallibly – fire on the first compression.

My car was built in an epoch when the Grand Fleet dominated the world's oceans. And under the bonnet, in the brass and the copper and the hugely overstrength componentry, there is much trace of marine influence. The factory record shows it going out to India, in Curzon's name (although I doubt he ever sat at the wheel).

Now the Grand Fleet is no more, and Lutyens' beautiful vistas in New Delhi have been overrun by shanty settlements. And yet, even when the Rolls was built brand new, 'there's something wrong with our bloody ships today'.*

It is the perennial problem, the need to arrest industrial decadence. At what point does the refusal of innovation overlap with the introduction of the 'black box'? – but not as an enhancement of quality, more a signpost to the soft life and 'shorter working hours'.

I drove for about forty minutes and on my return took a jug of iced lime juice and soda water to the music room where I played the piano, quite competently, until the light faded. A day filled with trivia, but *douceur de vivre* also.

---

* Admiral Beatty at Jutland when he lost three battlecruisers, due in part to the inferiority of their armour and the accuracy of the German fire-control systems.

Driving anywhere can be satisfying but for true enjoyment you can't beat the mountains

Having spent most of his life driving at speed on the country roads of England and Scotland, as well as on many throughout the Continent, Alan notes that the Stelvio Pass in Italy is really tough on cars. But his most memorable roads are those winding through the Dolomites. He drove his Rolls-Royce Silver Ghost along this route in the 1993 Commemorative Alpine Rally where great fun was had dicing with the other competitors.

The celebrities he refers to here include Frederick Forsyth, Noel Edmonds and David Steel, who were interviewed about their classic cars for this issue of Classic Cars.

Personally, I'm all in favour of celebrities being part of The Movement. They give us glamour, vitality and good public relations. They do quite a lot for values and generally keeping the hobby and sport which we all cherish in the public eye. They also allow (some of) us to enjoy a private sense of virtue. After all, we love our cars for what they are, don't we? We're not interested in them as male jewellery or pulling them around on trailers.

Mind you, I doubt if many of us would go as far as one of the world's pre-eminent celebrities, the venerable Mr Warren Buffett, chairman of Hathaway Securities Inc and the richest man in the USA after Bill Gates. He still drives himself around in a 1964 Impala convertible, usually with the top up.

I am not saying every celebrity doesn't know how to drive. Nick Mason (of Pink Floyd) really understands his cars and they give of their best to him. I happen to know this as he still owns my old D-type, XKD 516, one of the best in existence. It is so original it has a wraparound single-seater cowl and no aero-screen for the passenger. I used it to cure the asthma of one of my infant sons. Fastest oxygen tent on wheels.

The moment we speak of driving brings me straight to the editor's question this month: 'What is your favourite driving road?' To answer this properly is so fundamental to our tools, tastes and energies that it really deserves an essay on its own.

A collection of classics should be like a bag of golf-clubs. There should be the right car, just as there should be the right club, for every situation (and mood). I have a little circuit of my own on which I like to road-test everything that people bring for my edification. It consists mainly of the part of the old A20 that, because it has long been superseded by the M20, carries hardly any traffic. It remains a very good driving road, with testing high-speed corners, changes of surface, light, shade and gradient – including the Kick Hill, whose summit offers a good test of nerve (do you lift off at 90, or not?)

My advantage is that I have known practically every gutter, drain, variation in camber and so on since I first used to drive along here, pitting my then-new XK120 against my brother's Aurelia GT. So this terrain still allows me to make valid comparisons: for example, how very tiresome and difficult a 2.3 Alfa – which apparently you can't buy for less than £1m. – is when under pressure.

Now, as to the matching of roads and cars. First, I'd say any classic will feel wonderful on the A9 in Scotland. Beautiful surface, incredible scenery, finely engineered curves, bridges and pieces of double track. But beware – the Highland Constabulary enforce the speed limit ruthlessly, and if you're doing 62 where the limit is 60, they'll pull you in. Even if you are a duchess, for this actually happened to a duchess of my acquaintance.

But to test your skills and really start to feel at one with the machinery you have to go to the mountains. As someone who has tested cars across the whole arc of the Alps, I would suggest the following matches of passes and cars for maximum enjoyment.

The Stelvio is the hardest of all. Most cars will get frightfully hot; the very best is the Porsche 550A, and 911s are quite fun too, but you must have an open one. You lose half the flavour and all the sights in a coupé.

Very, very steep is the Vurzenpass. I don't think there is a car built that will get to the top of this without boiling.

The best combination of challenge and scenic beauty is undoubtedly the Dolomites. I drove my own Alpine Silver Ghost all over the best bits in the 1993 Commemorative Rally and took full advantage of the skimpy coachwork, 7.4 litre torque and high driving position to record some memorable times.

There are many favourite driving roads but if you get attached to a car and it, being a living creature, knows that you love it, it will give you satisfaction wherever you are. Whether or not you may be a 'celebrity'.

A wide selection of cars are needed to perfectly match all driving conditions

Alan rightly points out the difference between simply travelling and actually driving for enjoyment or sport. Driving should be intimate and involving where 'feel' is essential to the experience. As ever, Alan includes some rather eccentric notions.

'Cars *are* getting better, you know.'

This from my younger son (the only recorded human being to have written off a Suburu in a straight line) when I expressed surprise that an otherwise rather dreary-looking vehicle was fitted with ABS as standard.

Well, yes. But is it impossibly fogeyish to say that 'better' means less fun to drive? Of course one has to distinguish between *driving* and *travelling*. When I use the car to go to Scotland or Kent, or from Kent to St Brie-en-Vineux, where we stow on board so many bottles of Sauvignon that the suspension actually deflects, I am travelling.

For travel I want silence, power, fresh air on my face, warm air on my feet. I want directional stability, automatic transmission and power-assisted everything. American cars of the fifties used to do most of this, and feel lovely and strong, too, which their successors don't. But they are really too slow on motorways now, being mechanically uncomfortable at over eighty. The old DS Citroëns were very good, too, although typically French assembly means that there is a lot of wind noise from seams and edges.

Today the Jaguar is almost the best, with more accurate steering than the Lexus, but the seating position is fractionally too low – I don't like counting the rivets on a TIR lorry's axle casing.

I suppose it has to be the Bentley Turbo. Or better still the

Continental R, which – on account of its more rigid structure – never gets scuttle shake.

But if you want to drive, then my specification is quite different. No servos, please. I want mechanical linkages *everywhere*, even, if possible, to the windscreen wipers. Come to think of it, under ideal conditions you shouldn't even have a windscreen; it ought to be flat, or you should be looking over a perspex cowl like on a D-type, or one of those Scagletti Testa Rossas of the early sixties.

I want to know, by feel, what the tyres are doing; how near they are to their adhesion limits in wet or dry. I like to judge the BMEP* of the engine at any given moment from the exhaust note under load. I love all the hundred different ways in which machinery can make itself felt, and communicate with its master.

Before cars got 'better' I used to *drive* the very long distances over which I now *travel*. I once took the SS 100 to Skye from Kent in a day, helped by the midnight sun. I was so exhausted on arrival that I slept for eighteen hours and missed the early start for a difficult traverse of the Black Cuillin.

I remember another drive from Calais to Aix. I was in my XK, a friend in a big-bore Jaguar Mark VI. Only very seldom could I get him out of my driving mirror, and on arrival I looked like Captain Oates just before leaving the tent, while my chum and his girlfriend were ready to go into dinner.

In towns of course, the requirements are different again. If you're in no special hurry and want to catch up on your backlog on the carphone more or less any automatic with decent ventilation will do. But if you are in a hurry . . . Cars, direct steering, demonstratively low capital value and a high driving position all help. A Jeep is quite good – the Land-Rover is fractionally too wide – but my favourite is an early left-hand-drive 2CV.

And here's an idiosyncracy. For driving in Britain I prefer to sit on the left. In the same way that you can get much more fun in the Alps with right-hand steering. The nearest thing I ever got to a good bike, with weather protection, was a LHD Porsche

---

* BMEP: brake mean efficiency pressure. A method of measuring engine power and efficiency.

550A. Precise steering and visibility of all four corners allowed it to be placed impossibly close to whatever was being overtaken (i.e. everything).

Since then I have always specified LHD for all my Porsches, first 356, then 911. It is true the 911 is a wee bit wider, but provided you run close enough to adjust the other guy's driving mirror as you go past you should get through. I say 'should'. All 'A' roads are thirty-two feet wide – minimum – so there's bags of room for traffic coming towards you to adjust.

And if, one day, I meet Mad Max, then they will just have time to put on my tombstone: 'He always went for the middle lane'.

Some of the best motoring has been through the Alps in the Silver Ghost

In these entries for the Motor Journal, *Alan records his adventures competing in the 1973 Alpine Rally, as well as the 1993 Commemorative run, both exclusively for Rolls-Royce Silver Ghosts. His Ghost was mechanically very good but he had the most rudimentary body fitted. At a push he could get away with calling it 'sporting coachwork' that cost almost nothing.*

1973 Alpine Rally
Silver Ghost Chassis 29PK Reg No OU4647

21 June

Saltwood to Dover via Folkestone (Alan and Jane) seventeen miles. Forced car through narrow gap in fencing in order to gain (prohibited) access to bypass. Wrenched spare wheel off mounting, tearing straps and damaging offside wing. Crossed Channel, and loaded car on train at Ostend.

22 June

Munich to Vienna via Salzburg. 255 miles. 10 a.m.–5 p.m. (including all stops). Throttles jammed open on autobahn, which became awkward as weather deteriorated. Stopped in [P]★ and fiddled about, transferring governor spring to leading throttle arm, which closed throttles all right, but only allowed ½ opening. 'Pressed on' to Vienna at about 65 mph in *blinding* rain for last 150 miles; wet and cold, though excellent lunch at Autobahn station Lindach.

★ Alan's way of referring to a parking bay off the autobahn.

23 June

Vienna round trip to Alps via Nicker Alp. 275 miles. 11 a.m.–5 p.m. Weather was poor to start with, but cleared gradually to sunshine by afternoon. Car ran beautifully (after having governor bob-weights greased by JH [Jonathan Harley] in morning). Totally dominated the other rally entrants, and never put a foot wrong. We really threw it around, passing the seven cars ahead of us on the Alp – in a gust of steam as one fan belt broke – and excited the admiration of the German crew in a Range Rover.

24 June

Vienna to Portesch (Klagenfurt) via Graz (lunch). 10.30 a.m.–6 p.m. Battery ignition disappeared on the autobahn. Stopped in a layby and inspected leads and fuses. Jane rightly suggested sabotage resulting from ill-feeling among those carved up in the Alps yesterday. Diernst man gave us a pull and after a bit it seemed to return. Held up all the way to Graz where, as fanbelt was slipping ludicrously, we had to 'behave badly' in the parade, passing people in great surging lunges and further compounding the 'bad impression' of yesterday, in an effort to keep the engine from boiling by passing cool air through it. Block aggravated by pointless compulsory detour to get clip-joint lapel pins from beautiful redhead. Cold lunch inadequate, but red wine flowed. Endless traffic in Klagenfurt road. Coil ignition again packed up, and drove last ½ on magneto to the accompaniment of much spatting and banging. Still first RR to arrive.

25 June

Portesch to Venice via Udine. Left late after much indecision. Frontier saturated with timber 'juggernauts', and totally blocked (queue five miles) in the other direction. Once over in Italy weather was deliciously warm. Motored along uneventfully on the autostrada with all gauges normal and car going beautifully.

27 June   Saltwood [retrospective diary entry]

Back this afternoon after a wonderful six-day holiday. Took the big twin-carburettor Ghost and blasted down the autobahn, joining up late with the RREC Alpine Rally, cruising in the mountains, streaking on the Nicker Alp, backgammon with Hicky Dunbar at Portesch, and then the last glorious twenty-four hours, thundering along the autobahn in delicious hot air to Venice. Stayed at the *Monaco* (possibly even in the same room where I got grey water with Malcolm Napier in 1949 and he got the telegram saying he had failed 'schools' and we went off in the [Austin] Sheerline to Yugoslavia).

Silver Ghost S1914 Ch 59 TW 'The Antique'
The 2nd (harder?) Alpine Commemorative 20 years on

Sunday, 20 June 1993 – Vienna to Salzburg.
Solo. 257 miles 7 a.m.–7.45 p.m.

The Antique was parked in the Schonbrunn gardens. Looking very 'macho' (as 'Dan' Meyer said) beside all the shiny show-offs. But I was secretly uneasy about the clanking or *clonking* noise. Alan, who was scrutineering, seemed dismissive of it however. In colonial, thundery heat I blundered about unpacking and reloading. Duncan Dickinson and 'Tony' stood about help-fully. I had a great venison and noodles and retired, to wake just before the 4.50 (3.50 UK) alarm call. I virtually missed breakfast due to 'losing' things in the bedroom – particularly RayBans which seem to have gone irrevocably – and dashed swearing and carrying four pieces of luggage to load up.

Typically, and an ominous precursor – I would guess – of what was to follow, we stood thummingly in line outside the Palace for some forty-five minutes before moving off. I soon became impatient, and by double-parking and out-accelerating people (not difficult as I weigh 35 cwt only) I soon caught up with John Kennedy in Radley's old blue 'Eagle' R587 and a nameless in a red Ghost (also quite quick). Quite soon we started to misfire, or rather *hesitate* which deteriorated into a full misfire. My spirits sank. Was it ignition?

At one point it seemed to recover when I jiggled with the Adjust-Retard lever. She was unhappy, though just firing on all six on the long straight out, where the Austro-Daimler cars used to be tested, and the hobgoblin in the red Ghost slowly drew ahead. In a moment of recovery, at the start of the scrutineering,

I surged past them exiting a hairpin; then she stuttered hideously and audibly as the cut-out was open. I was thoroughly out-of-sorts. But I filled the tank and (over-) filled the radiator. Thereafter, fingers crossed, she gave no trouble and behaved beautifully, triumphantly when I swung out and passed Radley, at the very outset, and had the satisfaction of his getting smaller and smaller in the mirror. As I overtook him he did *not* acknowledge, but muttered to himself as we swept ahead.

Was in buoyant form as far as [Wels?] (arrived in rain) en fête. But reasonable lunch in marquee – ruthlessly barging to get ahead of queue. But after lunch rained very disagreeably and continuously. I stopped to put on more and more clothing. Got to Salzburg by the back route (unchanged) re-fuelling at the autobahn junction and getting angst about her restarting. Dodged an obviously pointless civic reception, and arrived by luck at the [Park?] Hotel to park in underground garage with all the other Ghosts. Triumphant at the high mileage, and glad of a rest day tomorrow.

Monday, 21 June – in Salzburg

Fiddled with the car a bit. Drove (late) to a boring reception outside the Civic Centre, peasants gawping. Car was leaking water massively and afterwards I found Alan who greased the water pump hugely – and cured it. Early start tomorrow. The engine 'clanks' objectionably, but Alan is calm. The car is really lovely to drive.

Tuesday, June 22 – Salzburg to Toblach (Tirol)

Left, in drizzle. Some difficulty and hesitation stops getting out of Salzburg. It's very hard navigating solo, and several times I overshot, had to reverse, left the indicator going on restarting, etc. etc. I know that if we could do the Tavern (long and steep) then she would do the Katschberg (even steeper, but shorter). Refreshed in Mauterndorf, poured in a lot of oil, but no water needed, thanks to Alan. Timed start, and she swooped off going splendidly though baulked by that slightly suspect Irish group going spastically slowly.

Two desirable and important cars (both of which I have owned, althou' one only briefly) are back on the market at about the same price of £220,000: the Bira, which was much mucked about by John Macdonald Hall – painted an acid blue instead of the lovely pale blue-grey of which I have got a few photos at Seend, seats recovered, B100 headlights and silly tail-lights – and which I saw without much longing on the Scottish rally. I drove it, found the power down and clutch slipping – but still the best handling and braking of all the Derbys.

Pinfold-like I complained about the badges and the starting handle, which was engraved AYM 300, being 'missing', but discovered them that evening in the cupboard. I had removed them before sale! Jane was doubtful. Didn't like the idea of putting in the Green Rolls (the wedding car), said 'you can't go back', this was the car of our days at Seend when the crumbs were young etc. I offered Charles 'paper' at *my* cost so that the car would in fact have cost me 225. The 'Alpine' and the J2 Allard and the Cad Coupé. But he only really wanted the Cad at 190. Typically he has four Ghosts and two J2 Allards in stock at the moment. But the realisation that I am locked into paper made me depressed, and disillusioned with the cars. Sometimes, like this morning, I looked wistfully at the static 'Mickey' 2CV under straw in the Stables, thought *that*, a 4¼, AC1800 and two Jag sports would about do me.

Later

After speaking to Charles, he offered to take 'works of art'. I faxed him copiously from the Phillips list, noting as I did so the huge amount of 'contents' that one needed to make up the value of one car.

When the going got tough, one car kept going – the magnificent Talbot Lago. Sadly this is where Alan Clark's engine management system shorted

This was the last column Alan wrote for Classic Cars. *He penned these words in the middle of July and died on 5 September 1999. Ion Trewin, his editor for the* Diaries, *thinks it is probably Alan's last piece of published writing.*

As usual it contains an amusing personal anecdote, here relating to a Talbot Lago as featured in the magazine; a keen knowledge of great racing cars in action over fifty years ago at Le Mans; mention of a good but obscure reference book; and thoughts on the ill-fated BRM V-16 engines. These are the writings of an erudite man who had experienced and really enjoyed some of the finest things in life, including some of the very best Vintage, historic, classic and contemporary cars.

His wife Jane has described him elsewhere as being 'an utter bastard, but I love him'. In many ways he should have been a reviled figure of envy, especially in the close-knit world of old cars. But his absolute love of machines, his passion for driving, his knowledge and understanding of the broadest canvases led to a great deal of respect. In the final analysis, Alan did the sort of things with cars that all enthusiasts dream of. He didn't keep a selection of pristine models locked up in an air-tight garage; he got out there and thrashed the trousers off his scruffy Bentleys, Jaguars, Porsches and Rolls-Royces. He had enormous fun and did it all with inimitable style.

In the 1940s and 1950s, three great laboratories helped the design of classic sports racing cars evolve. For engine design, the Le Mans Twenty-Four Hours was the most important (most engines pack up by the time they reach the Mulsanne hairpin at the end of one of Europe's longest flat-out runs, with oil like marmalade). Key tests of brakes and suspension were the Alpine Rally and, more importantly, because it included a general test of how tightly the car has been bolted together, the Liège–Rome–Liège.

I have a particular respect for any car that could perform with distinction on that one. This is rooted, I suppose, in what I saw of the road conditions in that region in 1946–7. Craters, broken bridges necessitating day tours on the river bed, wrecked and flooded pavé and poor street lighting (once it was needed) combined to make motoring quite unpleasant.

A fellow subaltern, attached to the British Mission in Trieste, used all his leave to drive to Yugoslavia and court his girlfriend, south of Belgrade. The car he took for this marathon (not for nothing did the Liège–Rome become known as the *marathon de la route*) was a Talbot-Lago 4½ litre. For three years, that car took punishment every weekend and never either wore out or broke.

Later, I watched the Lagos wipe out at Le Mans, until finally being caught out by the failure of Levegh to change up to top. This was on the Mulsanne straight where, in 1951, Lagos finally met their nemesis when the C-type Jaguars slid past at more than 120 mph. Inevitable if you spoil the aerodynamics of a single-seater Grand Prix car with cycle fenders and lighting equipment.

I have always been addicted to the cubic inch theory and to putting big engines in light frames where they will work obediently without undue stress. At the opposite pole of automotive design is the 16-cylinder BRM. Here, the designers made the understandable mistake of looking at the competition and deciding the easiest way to beat it would be to imitate and make it better.

At this point in GP development the dominant cars were all Italian and the essence of Italian technical excellence is fragility. Unfortunately, the reality of sixteen aluminium coffee cups going up and down 8000 times a minute was doomed. I always thought the Lagos would have demolished the 16-cylinder BRMs in combat; and certainly once Gonzales started to mix it in the 4½ litre 12-cylinder Ferrari, the fate of the BRM was sealed.

A pity, because in many ways the 16-cylinder engine was the apotheosis of a particular design philosophy, half Italian in concept, half Japanese, which would have effectively translated, together with its operational lessons, into commercial application in later generations of specialized performance cars.

This is one of the appeals of the classic for many. The driver can actually feel the genes of cars that have been built late on and acquired a reputation for excellence. Part of the fun is to spot some of them coming towards you. Some, of course, never make it, like the NSU Wankel. Was this not to be the great performance car of the future but actually turned out a dead loss?

Anyone doubting the intrinsic merit of the 4½ litre Lago should read Duncan Hamilton's *Touch Wood*, where he extols both its brute power and magnificent handling. Richard Pilkington, who drove one brilliantly, says, 'If you get into difficulties on a corner, just find the right place in the book – it'll tell you what to do – and do it.'

Many sports racing cars with huge engines are disappointing. They can be nose-heavy and the power often fails to come in when you need it. But most Lagos had a Wilson pre-selector gearbox – a dream device, because you can select the next gear in advance and just pump the clutch when you need it.

I never took to the Lamborghini. It did not really perform in competition, but its origin was noble, arising from personal rivalry between Lamborghini and Ferrari. When two rich men are out to do each other down, they spend money freely. For enthusiasts, this usually presents an opportunity. Consider the benefits for us over a decade from the rivalry between William Lyons of Jaguar and David Brown of Aston Martin. Who now will take their place?

The end

Poignant stuff, this is Alan Clark not long before he died. Here he is too ill and exhausted to write so he is dictating his thoughts to Jane. He's trying to tell his beloved wife how best to dispose of his cars, except he doesn't really manage it. All he can do is say how much he loves them all, some of which he has enjoyed driving for over fifty years, most of which have nicknames.

His tragic opening line leads on to what he refers to as a 'cull list'. He goes on to discuss the cars in intimate detail, clearly having to break off occasionally as his emotions get the better of him. A sad and premature end to an exciting life lived to the full but fortunately leaving us with some great motoring words and memories.

Tape Undated

Absolutely *blissful* afternoon. Everything is so lovely. And this morning I did two amazing things, helped by Jane ... went down and supervised while she got the C-type going, which she did perfectly, then sat while the white duck was helped out of the conker tree door. An absolutely *lovely* pair of Saltwood things.

It made me all very, very sad somehow because I fear that this is something that's over for me, and I can't quite get back into the groove of sort of looking...

I've already said this is the beginning of the cull list ... not cull list, checklist that may have got lost.

Priorities and what one has to look at:

(1) Obviously the white XK120. Owned by me since 1950. Brand new. The only one owner since new in the world.

Initially prepared by the factory for the Carrera Panamericana. Lot of stuff in the file, this and that, what's been
done to it.

(2) The Silver Ghost Alpine. The famous car that ran rings
round everybody in the Alpine Rally and starting procedures
and so on, you know, are all in the armrest, but basically you
know the bat mascot, it's very famous and well known and
got an 1852 axle which is important, it's not the year built,
it's the ... makes it very, very high, very high for a Ghost,
and high compression pistons and something I have written
here ... board notes ... don't understand what that is. But
I would tend to avoid selling that either, I think it's a sort of
Saltwood, like piece of the Saltwood furniture.

(3) The New Bing (Bentley Continental S1). Well, we all know
about the New Bing. Bought new in 1958. Been with us
through everything even, longer than Lillian, say. Or James.
No, James was just alive when we got it because it was ...
it's a 1958 car bought in 1960. Two little points about the
New Bing, it had a ... it's now got a very, very high correct
axle. For a long time it was on a slightly lower axle which is
somewhere in Bob's room in the cardboard box, which
made it very, very much faster, because of its wonderful
close-ratio box. The suspension has been done and it's pretty
good generally. In addition to the axle possibly being changed
back it needs a new bottom gear and there is a brand-new
bottom gear also in the box in Bob's room and P & A Wood
will put in.

(4) And the next one is the green R-type Continental which is
a very special car. Christian Hueber is writing the *catalogue*
of R-type Continentals and was very taken by it and he is
writing a lot about it in his book. And it's actually a very
nice sort of classy private classic, just drive/ride about.

(5) Now a very difficult car which has got a very special cachet,
that's the green Buick Roadmaster convertible, which is
the archetypal thing that classic Americans want ... shift.
Everything works, is brand new, under 20,000 miles, it really

has. And it just wants beautiful cleaning and detailing and waxing.

(6) The Chapron, that's for Mummy, of course. It belongs to her completely. We always use it for holidays. It just needs more using really. It's extremely pleasing. A genuine original one like that bought new by Jane and all the papers and every detail on it is minimum £60.

(7) Now a big conundrum. A Derby. Its chassis number, 91MX, which makes a very, very late gearbox car . . . on the Vanden Plas tourer rather like the Bira. It is *unusually* rare and import-ant on this car – I think there are only three others. And of course, it needs more attention. I haven't even Connollised, cleaned and washed off the seats. It's still at P & A Wood. The wings need painting and endless things. It's . . . an awful lot of money has gone into it but don't get exhausted and dump it because I know Derbys . . . it actually drives and handled better than a lot of Derbys too. Nicer ride. Nicer steering. And it is unusually rare and important.

(8) On the other scale of Derbys, the Barnato car. It floods sometimes. You can try switching the ignition on and off . . . off and then again it will clear itself. It's halfway through a restoration, fatal thing, well, not a full restoration wouldn't . . . do that, tart up. And all the wood . . . not all the wood cappings but the missing wood cappings are either in the winter office or in . . . holdings shed on the left, I think there may be one on the shelf there, or there might still be one in the long garage but I rather doubt it.
I am closing this now for a minute.

(9) Right. I'm going to pick it up with the King George V car. Because that is where the wood cappings are for the Barnato car, a lot of them are on the back seat in the King George V car. And the point I must make about the King George V car is that it is exceptionally rare. It's a 1914 Silver Ghost, chassis 20UB, the very best year, for Silver Ghosts and . . . so you go right back into timelessness. And it is, it's gotta be marketed very carefully. It was . . . it's got a cranked gear

lever because it started off life with a touring body so the gear lever, which was a factory option, cranks in so as you don't have to put your hand out of the window to change gear with narrow bodies which follows the roll of the body. Now the other thing that is important about the King George V car is why it's called the King George V car, because it was sent to Canada in 1914 and it was used by George V to review the Canadian Division in Flanders in 1916 or 1917 and there is actually a picture in some of the Rolls literature of him doing that. So that gives it an extra cachet.

Afterword Jane Clark

A major role in my life

I have loved helping with this book. I can go to the Long Garage now and talk to the cars as Al used to, but for a year I found it the place which upset me the most. It was impossible even to unlock the doors. The cars meant so much to him and his knowledge and love of them all, and now the place was still and they were just sitting silently deteriorating in the dampness of the garage – damp because Al had cut holes in the doors – the top holes to let in the robins and the swallows who nested there and the lower holes for any small mammals at any time they should choose, which as you can imagine resulted in some of the cars containing the unmistakable signs of mouse droppings. Once memorably the cloth headlining of the Barnato Bentley which was not much driven had a really beautifully constructed bird's nest made in it which worried Al not a bit – he thought it showed what taste she had.

Cars played a major role in my life with Al, starting in Rye with the XK120 which I can still hear accelerating down the straight from Winchelsea on a summer evening before we were married – the change of note as it hit the cobbles at the bottom of Mermaid Street and the slow rumbling roar as it passed our house on its way to Watchbell Street where Al lived. It is still here in the garage quite unchanged, along with the old grey VW which Al raced in hill climbs and I learnt to drive on and passed my test in before it had a Porsche engine. We went on our honeymoon in it and after going round the First World War French battlefields (Al was at the time writing *The Donkeys*) we drove on to the Nurburgring for the German Grand Prix.

When we were first married cars came and went. We were

broke, Al could never resist a profit, and we simply had no garaging space – we never have had enough space and even now, a year and a half after Al's death, my Discovery sits out. This is unfortunate as it appears not to be waterproof. Once 'Ruby', the Austin Seven, spent over a year in the hall of my in-laws' bungalow, but not while they were alive, for although we collected cars in the same way as they did pictures they did not see them as art.

The rule used to be no more unless something goes, but Al got round this by buying what had caught his eye and having work done on it at once so the new chassis number on a bill would be the first I would know of it. We all used to make cull lists, only six cars were to remain, but we simply could not agree. The boys liked the fast and dangerous ones that were on my list so they won. It was impossible to have favourites as each had its own quite different appeal. My Citroën Decapotable and the grey Continental were always on my keep list. I loved, too, the Silver Ghost in which we did the Alpine Rally. A really comfortable car, but strictly for good weather like the C-type.

We all became experts in towing. Most fine weekends Al would disappear towards the Long Garage saying as he passed – 'I'm just going to hitch up the Discovery. Can you come down in five minutes to give me a pull?' A series of arm signals became necessary as anyone who tows with a diesel knows the noise it makes means you cannot always hear if the car behind has fired. Another job that fell to me was to hold a pad over the intake of the C type to enable it to start without sucking in cold air – I hated this as the great engine would make terrifying bangs and sparks and I was convinced it was going to explode and catch fire.

Batteries were and still are a complete nightmare. The place is littered with dead ones which would no longer take a charge, and most of Al's rough shirts have battery acid holes in them as he carried them from car to car. Why are all cars not fitted with on/off switches like the Porsche? I know you should take off the leads if you leave the cars standing, but we never did. Try finding the Continental's battery. No, it is not in the engine compartment, but under the carpet in the boot and impossible to get at, or under the back seat. Unlike the Ghost, where it is beautifully housed in a box on the running board.

In the early days and when he had time Al loved cleaning the cars. Vintage Bentley leather seats are easy to remove to work on inside, likewise large chrome lights. However, much work was done in the garages, and all kinds of household items would take on fresh roles. Only recently I found a long-lost jam thermometer down there, hanging on a nail.

He was very good at keeping up with the prices of cars. We used to sit with the sale catalogues and he would guess how much each one had gone for and I would tell him whether he had bought it or not as I was in charge of the prices sold list. He kept nearly every car magazine and the house is full of them dating back to the 1940s – including bound volumes of *Motor Sport* and *Car Illustrated*. Ion and I found a wonderful selection of them in the very top tower.

The cars he loved were as original as possible and weathered by use. He hated anything over restored. He would go down to the Long Garage on fine evenings and sit by the cars writing up his journal at a rough desk. Just to be with some of the things he loved most was, as he used to say, a form of therapy. And the future? I will make the cull list with the boys, but with four grandsons growing up we will have to be quick in case one of them has inherited his grandfather's addiction. Indeed I think it may be too late.

Saltwood
April 2001